French
grammar handbook

Alan Moys

Berlitz Publishing Company, Inc.
Princeton   Mexico City   Dublin   Eschborn   Singapore

French Grammar Handbook

Copyright © 1993 Alan Moys

Published by Berlitz Publishing Company, Inc.
400 Alexander Park, Princeton, NJ 08540 USA
9-13 Grosvenor St., London W1X 9FB UK

Berlitz Trademark Reg. U.S. Patent Office and other countries –
Marca Registrada

Reprinted June 1998
Printed in Canada
ISBN 2-8315-6387-9

The Author:

Alan Moys is an experienced teacher and author of French textbooks. He was formerly director of CILT, the Centre for Information on Language Teaching and Research in London.

The Series Editor:

Christopher Wightwick was formerly principal inspector of Modern Languages for England and UK representative on the Council of Europe Modern Languages Project.

CONTENTS

How to use this Handbook

This *Grammar Handbook* can be used in two ways.

• If you want to get a general picture of some aspect of French grammar, start with the introductory list of *Contents*. You can then read through the relevant sections of the text. The many cross-references will lead you to other, related topics.

• If you want to find out more about a specific grammatical point or about the use of particular French words or expressions, consult the extensive *Index* at the end of the book. The *Index* has many subheadings, and in addition items are frequently referenced under more than one heading. The *Index* will point you to individual paragraph numbers.

The *Handbook* gives a great deal of information about grammatical forms and structures, but above all is designed to show how they fit in with what you want to say or write.

• Grammatical terms are treated as convenient labels and used whenever necessary, but the *Handbook* does not assume that you already know what they mean. All the sections of this book include explanations of grammatical terms.

• A key feature is the number of examples, drawn from a wide stock of French in current use. Wherever it makes sense to do so, these examples are linked together into a short dialogue, topic, or narrative. If you do not understand a grammatical explanation, the example will help you to recognize the feature.

• This *Handbook* is intended for people who want to *use* their French. Where constructions or expressions are used only in formal contexts, this is made clear in the text.

Finally, as a safety net, there are special warning sections wherever you see this sign, to help you avoid the more obvious traps and pitfalls.

A
PUTTING IDEAS INTO WORDS

1 Classes of words, parts of speech

1a *What kind of word is it?*

It is often impossible to say what class a word belongs to (what *part of speech* it is) until it is used in a sentence. On the other hand, understanding a sentence, especially in another language, may well depend on knowing what part of speech a word is, so it is useful to be able to recognize them. In this *Handbook* we define each part of speech mainly by what it *does* – what it refers to and its function and position in the sentence. If you can also recognize it by its form, for example, from its endings, then this is described as well.

In the following paragraphs we will look briefly at the main classes of words, give their English and French names, some examples, and references to the paragraphs in the book where they are first defined.

1b *Content words*

Four classes of word (the *content words*) contain most of the meaning of the sentence:

(i) *Verbs (les verbes)*

J'*apprends* le français; je *parle*, je *lis*, j'*écris* la langue.	I *am learning* French; I *speak*, *read*, and *write* the language.

➤ [For more on verbs ➤PART C.]

(ii) *Nouns (les substantifs)*

J'aime la *France*, sa *culture*, sa *langue*, ses *paysages*, ses *villes*, et son *peuple*.	I like *France*, its *culture*, its *language*, its *scenery*, its *towns*, and its *people*.

[For more on nouns ➤18.]

(iii) Adjectives (**les adjectifs**)

La France est un pays *riche, cultivé, varié,* **et** *progressif.*	France is a *rich, cultured, diverse,* and *progressive* country.

[For more on adjectives ➤20.]

(iv) Adverbs (**les adverbes**)

On trouve *facilement* **des journaux français à New York, et je vois** *souvent* **des films français.**	You can *easily* find French newspapers in New York, and I *often* see French movies.

[For more on adverbs ➤24.]

1c Structure words

Structure words do add to the meaning, of course, but they do it mainly by the way they relate to the content words.

(i) Auxiliary verbs (**les verbes auxiliaires**)

The verbs **avoir** and **être** are used with other verbs to create a range of compound tenses.

J'*ai* **été deux fois à Marseille. J'y** *suis* **allé pour la première fois en 1970.**	I've been to Marseille twice. I went there for the first time in 1970.

[For more on auxiliary verbs ➤7c, 11b, 11c, 17e.]

(ii) Pronouns (**les pronoms**)

Pronouns substitute for nouns, often to avoid unnecessary repetition:

Je **compte beaucoup de Français parmi mes amis.** *Je leur* **écris, et** *je* **vois souvent** *ceux qui* **habitent Los Angeles.** *On se* **parle souvent au téléphone.**	*I* number a lot of French people among my friends. *I* write to *them,* and *I* often see *those who* live in Los Angeles. *We* often talk on the telephone.

3

[For more on pronouns ➤21.]

(iii) Determiners *(les déterminants)*

Determiners include some of the most common words in any language, such as the articles (**un, une, des, le, la, les**), the demonstratives (**ce, cette, ces**), and the possessives (**mon, ma, mes, son, sa, ses,** etc.).

[For more on determiners ➤19.]

(iv) Prepositions *(les prépositions)*

Prepositions are connecting words placed in front of nouns or their equivalent. They include words like **pour** (for), **devant** (in front of), **avec** (with), **dans** (in).

[For more on prepositions ➤23.]

(v) Conjunctions *(les conjonctions)*

Conjunctions are used to join clauses, phrases, or words. The most common conjunctions are **et** (and), **mais** (but), **ou** (or).

[For more on conjunctions ➤5a.]

(vi) Exclamations *(les exclamations)*

Exclamations express sudden and strong emotions of all sorts, in a single word or phrase such as **Quel dommage!, Mon Dieu!** or **Flûte, alors!**

[For more on exclamations ➤22.]

② Getting it down on paper: spelling and punctuation

This chapter describes the basic features of French spelling and punctuation. It does not deal directly with pronunciation, as attempts to describe sounds on paper are more likely to be a hindrance than a help.

2a *The French alphabet*

(i) The letters of the alphabet are the same in French as in English. They are listed below, together with their pronunciation using normal French pronunciation, and spelling conventions. It is helpful to be able to use the French alphabet when spelling names and addresses on the telephone, etc.

A a	**H** ache as in	**N** enne	**U** u
B bé	acheter	**O** o	**V** vé
C cé	**I** i	**P** pé	**W** double vé
D dé	**J** ji	**Q** cu	**X** ikse
E euh or é	**K** ka	**R** ère	**Y** i grec
F effe	**L** elle	**S** esse	**Z** zède
G gé	**M** emme	**T** té	

• When spelling aloud:

Comment cela s'écrit-il?	How do you spell that? (How is it
Comment ça s'écrit?	written?)
Pourriez-vous me l'épeler?	Could you spell it for me?

B majuscule	capital B
petit c	small c
deux p	double p

The letter **h** is never sounded as in English. However, there are two categories of **h** in French, the difference being not in their pronunciation but in their effect on words preceding them if they end in a vowel.

Where the initial **h** is classified (in the dictionary) as a mute **h**, the word is treated as though it begins with a vowel. So rather than **le homme** or **le hôtel** you find **l'homme** and **l'hôtel**.

Where the **h** is classified as an **h** aspirate, no elision is made before a vowel: **la haie** and **le hêtre**.

(ii) Capital letters

Capital letters are used less often in French than in English, although the overall pattern of their use in punctuation is similar. Capital letters are not used in French in the following cases:

- Days of the week and months of the year [➤28a]:

mardi, le 20 décembre	Tuesday, December 20th

- Adjectives of nationality, including names of languages:

Une voiture allemande.	A German car.
Cette lettre est en espagnol.	This letter is in Spanish.

A capital letter is required when adjectives of nationality are used as a noun to mean *a German, an English woman* etc.:

Il y a des Anglais dans l'hôtel.	There are some English people in the hotel.

- Nouns relating to places and used as part of the place name:

le boulevard St Michel	St Michel Boulevard
la rue de Rivoli	Rivoli Road
la Mer Noire	the Black Sea

- Points of the compass:

le nord, le sud, l'ouest, l'est, le nord-est, etc.

But **le Nord** (name of **département**).

- Personal status and professions in titles:

le docteur Dubois	Doctor Dubois
le général Martin	General Martin
monsieur et madame Arthaud	Mr. and Mrs. Arthaud

- Proper names widely adopted as standard names of products:

le bordeaux, le beaujolais	wines
le gruyère, le hollande	cheeses
le scotch	adhesive tape (not scotch whisky!)

(iii) *Accents in French*

The accents used in French have the following names:

´	**accent aigu**	acute accent
`	**accent grave**	grave accent
^	**(accent) circonflexe**	circumflex
ç	**cédille**	cedilla
¨	**tréma**	diaeresis

• When the letter **e** is spelled aloud with any accent (acute, grave, or circumflex), it is pronounced **è accent grave**, **é accent aigu**, etc.
• The cedilla occurs only with the letter **c** and in spelling aloud is **c cédille**.
• Accents are usually omitted with capital letters.

(iv) *Accents in pronunciation and spelling*

Accents serve two purposes in French, one useful, the other only marginally so. The useful purpose is to indicate pronunciation, as when we distinguish the word **donné** from the word **donne**. The second purpose distinguishes words that have identical spelling but different meanings, such as **des** (some) and **dès** (from) or **où** (where) and **ou** (or). In these cases the presence of the accent has no effect on the pronunciation.

(A) Accents on **e**

The only vowel whose pronunciation is affected by the addition of an accent is **e**.

• An acute accent on an **e** always has the same effect:

donné has the same sound as **donner**

• A grave accent on an **e** is almost always a pronunciation marker, the pronunciation being different from the **é** acute:

père, mère, dernière	all rhyme with	**paire**
parallèle, modèle, Michèle	all rhyme with	**elle**

The above examples illustrate an important spelling rule in French. When a word ends in **e** + consonant + **e**, the first **e** must have a grave accent or the consonant must be doubled. Both forms are common and have identical pronunciation:

Mère, terre, complète, emplette

(B) The presence of an acute, grave, or circumflex accent on the other vowels (**a**, **i**, **o**, or **u**) can generally be ignored in pronunciation, though of course they are required to produce correct written language. French abounds with these largely redundant accents (for example **crû** and **cru**). Often they mark the disappearance of a letter from the spelling of a word like **forêt** (forest) or **étable** (stable).

(C) The cedilla placed under a **c** before **a**, **o**, or **u** means that the **c** is to be pronounced **s** and not **k**:

leçon, reçu, commençait

A **c** before **e** or **i** is always pronounced as an **s** – as in **cité** and **recevoir**.

(D) A diaeresis (¨) over a letter indicates that the vowel on which it is placed is separated in pronunciation from the vowel preceding it:

Noël   Christmas   **Moïse**   Moses

2b   *Punctuation*

(i)   *Punctuation marks*

The principal punctuation marks in French are:

.	**le point**	period, full stop
,	**la virgule**	comma
;	**le point-virgule**	semi-colon
:	**deux points**	colon
?	**le point d'interrogation**	question mark
!	**le point d'exclamation**	exclamation mark
-	**le trait (d'union)**	hyphen
—	**le tiret**	dash
...	**points de suspension**	. . .
()	**les parenthèses** (feminine)	brackets, parentheses
<< >> *or*		
"..."	**les guillemets** (masculine)	inverted commas, quotation marks

(A) Quotation marks

The conventions for the punctuation of direct speech in French are different from English. Inverted commas are often omitted altogether, or are included only at the start and finish of an exchange of direct speech. A dash is widely used to open direct speech:

—**Venez donc ce soir!**   "Come this evening, then!"

Adding the speaker does not entail closing and reopening the direct speech with formal punctuation marks:

—**Venez donc ce soir, répondit**   "Come this evening, then,"
Christophe, à partir de huit   Christophe replied, "from eight
heures.   o'clock onwards."

(B) The comma

The use of the comma is for the most part the same as in English. However, in presenting numbers there are important differences.

In French a comma is used in decimals where in English there would be a decimal point (i.e., a period):

L'inflation est de 3,8%.   Inflation is at 3.8%.

Commas are not used with large numbers in French [➤26]. A gap is left where in English there would be a comma:

43 000 personnes   43,000 people

Linking words together

3a Compound words or phrases?

All languages need ways of combining word meanings so as to express more complex ideas. This may be done either by joining two words together to form one (possibly hyphenated) compound word, or by linking separate words to form phrases.

3b Compound words and the use of hyphens

One frequently finds two words linked directly by a hyphen in French to form a new meaning. Verb-noun combinations are common:

un porte-monnaie	purse
un gratte-ciel	skyscraper
un pare-chocs	car fender/ bumper
un tire-bouchon	corkscrew
un essuie-glace	windshield wiper

Other combinations include noun + noun, preposition + noun, verb + adverb:

une porte-fenêtre	french window(s)
un chou-fleur	cauliflower
un hors-bord	outboard motor
un passe-partout	skeleton key

[For formation of plurals of compound nouns ➤18e(iii).]

3c Phrases expressing a complex idea

In English the words *ball* and *golf* are both nouns, but in the expression *golf ball*, the noun *golf* is used as an attributive adjective. The French language also makes use of nouns (and the infinitive form of verbs) in this way, but the wordings are different. When a noun is used as an adjective, it follows the noun it describes, and generally requires a linking preposition such as **de**, **à**, or **en**:

une balle de golf	a golf ball
une tasse à café	a coffee cup
une montre en or	a gold watch

De is the most widely used link in these formulations:

une maison de campagne	a country house
un match de football	a football game
les maladies d'hiver	winter ailments

Although there are many exceptions, **à** here tends to be used to convey the notion of purpose or function:

une boîte aux lettres	a mailbox	(a box for letters)
une salle à manger	a dining room	(a room for eating)
une table à repasser	an ironing board	(a table for ironing)

En is generally used to indicate "made of" or "in the shape of":

un tabouret en chêne	an oak stool
une veste en cuir	a leather jacket
un escalier en spirale	a spiral staircase

Note the distinction in meaning between phrases of the following type:

une tasse à café	a coffee cup
une tasse de café	a cup of coffee
une boîte à allumettes	a matchbox
une boîte d'allumettes	a box of matches

B
PUTTING A SENTENCE TOGETHER

Recognizing sentences

4a   What is a sentence?

A sentence is a spoken or written utterance that has a subject and a predicate. When talking we often say things that are not sentences (for example, exclamations [➤22] or isolated phrases that make perfect sense because we know the context), but in writing we usually try to use complete sentences. The way a sentence is put together is known as its *syntax*.

4b   The subject of a sentence

(i)   What is a subject?

Generally speaking the subject is the word or phrase whose action or state the sentence is describing:

Le *ferry* part de Douvres à sept heures.	The *ferry* leaves Dover at seven o'clock.

The subject of the sentence is **ferry**, and the main verb is **part**.

***Nous* sommes heureux de partir en vacances.**	*We* are happy to be going on vacation.

The subject of the sentence is **nous** and the main verb is **sommes**.

Sometimes the subject of a verb does not refer to anything in particular:

Il pleut.	It is raining.

Here, the subject is **il** (it), and is known as an impersonal subject.

(ii)   Passive sentences

The verb may be used in a form known as the *passive* [➤15], which means that the subject of the verb, instead of doing the action of the verb, becomes the receiver of the action:

Tous les passagers **sont accueillis par l'équipe du bateau.**	*All the passengers* are welcomed by the crew of the ship.

The subject of the sentence is **tous les passagers** and the main verb is **sont accueillis**, which is the passive form of **accueillir**. The welcoming is done not by the subject, but by **l'équipe**.

(iii)   *Omission of the subject*

Sometimes the subject is omitted but understood. This happens in command forms [➤13]:

Prenez vos places dans le restaurant, s'il vous plaît.	Take your places in the restaurant, please.

Here the main verb is **prenez**, and the subject – understood but not stated – is **vous**.

4c   The predicate of a sentence

The predicate consists of the whole of the rest of the sentence, excluding the subject. It must have at least a main verb, that is, a verb in one of the simple tenses [➤11b]. This verb *agrees* with the subject; that is, its form changes to match the subject:

Le bateau arrive.	The ship arrives.

Here **arrive** agrees with **le bateau**, which is in the third person singular: *he*, *she*, or *it* in English [➤21b].

Les passagers regagnent leurs voitures.	The passengers return to their vehicles.

In this case **regagnent** is in the third person plural to agree with the plural subject **les passagers**. The predicate consists of **regagnent** plus the remainder of the sentence, which in this case is the direct object **leurs voitures** [➤8b]. However, most predicates have more than the minimum requirement of a main verb: the above illlustration could equally have included, for example, an adverbial phrase [➤24] such as:

| **Les passagers regagnent leurs voitures *avec impatience*.** | The passengers return to their vehicles *impatiently*. |

4d   Types of sentence

There are three types of complete sentence:

- statements, which are the basic form;
- direct questions [➤6];
- commands [➤13].

All three types must have a main clause; they may also have any number of subordinate clauses.

4e   Main clauses and subordinate clauses

(i)   Main clauses

A main clause is the key grammatical element of a sentence, to which any other parts are connected. It can often stand by itself, though of course it may not make much sense on its own. The main clause does not necessarily open the sentence, though it often does. Here is a sentence in the form of a single main clause:

| **Les Robinson cherchent une boulangerie.** | The Robinsons look for a bakery. |

Now the sentence becomes the main clause in a longer sentence:

| **Une fois qu'ils sont sortis du port, les Robinson ont cherché une boulangerie, parce qu'ils adorent le pain français.** | Once they are out of the dock area, the Robinsons look for a bakery, because they love French bread. |

The main clause is still **les Robinson cherchent une boulangerie**, but there are now two *subordinate clauses*, each adding information about the main clause. (The first subordinate clause says *when* the Robinsons go in search of a baker's, and the second says *why*.)

(ii)   Subordinate clauses

A subordinate clause is always dependent on a main clause,

whose meaning it completes or expands. It is linked to the main clause by one of three types of word:

• a subordinating conjunction (such as **une fois que** and **parce que** in the above illustration);
• a question word, such as **où** (where), **pourquoi** (why), **quand** (when), or **combien** (how much) [➤6d]:

John Robinson demande à un passant *où* **se trouve la boulangerie la plus proche.**	John Robinson asks a passerby *where* the nearest bakery is.

(The main clause is followed by a subordinate clause introduced by **où**.)

• a relative pronoun such as **qui** (who/which), or **que** (whom/which) [➤21j]:

Le passant, *qui* **habite le quartier, donne les indications au visiteur anglais.**	The passerby, *who* lives in the neighborhood, gives directions to the English visitor.

This example reminds us that – exactly as in English – a main clause is often split in two by the insertion of a subordinate clause, in this case **qui habite le quartier,** which gives us additional information about **le passant**.

Linking clauses together

5a Clauses with conjunctions

Conjunction means "joining." There are two sorts of conjunction, *coordinating* and *subordinating*. Their names reflect their function in the sentence.

(i) Coordinating conjunctions

Coordinating conjunctions link clauses of equal status: main with main, subordinate with subordinate. They tell us something about how the clauses' meanings relate to each other (reinforcing, contrasting, etc.), but do not change the status of the clauses relative to each other:

Les Robinson achètent leur pain et se mettent en route.	The Robinsons buy their bread and set off on their journey.

Here two main clauses are linked by the simplest of conjunctions, **et** (and).

The principal coordinating conjunctions in French are:

et	and	**ou**	or
mais	but	**donc**	therefore, so

Il fait gris *mais* il ne pleut pas.	The weather is dull *but* it isn't raining. (*main + main, linked by* **mais**)
Est-ce que les Robinson vont prendre l'autoroute, *ou* est-ce qu'ils préfèrent les petites routes tranquilles?	Will the Robinsons take the highway, *or* do they prefer the quieter back roads? (*main + main, linked by* **ou**)

(ii) Subordinating conjunctions

Subordinating conjunctions link subordinate clauses to the rest of the sentence. Usually the subordinate clause is the equivalent of an adverbial expression [➤24]. Some subordinating conjunctions are followed by the subjunctive in French [➤14], others by an indicative form of the verb [➤12]:

Puisqu'ils ne sont pas pressés, ils décident de prendre les petites routes.	Since they are not in a hurry, they decide to take the back roads. (*subordinate clause after* **puisque** + *present indicative* **sont**)
Afin que les enfants puissent mieux apprécier la campagne, les parents décident de prendre les petites routes.	So that the children can see more of the countryside, their parents decide to take the back roads. (*subordinate clause after* **afin que** + *present subjunctive* **puissent**)

(iii)   In the following list of frequently used subordinating conjunctions, those that normally require a subjunctive are preceded by (**S**):

S	**à condition que**	on condition that
S	**afin que**	in order that
	ainsi que	just as (*comparison*)
	alors que	when, whereas
	à mesure que	(*progressively*) as
S	**à moins que**	unless
	après que	after
	aussitôt que	as soon as
S	**avant que**	before
S	**bien que**	although
	comme	as (when *or* because)
	dès que	as soon as
S	**de façon que**	so that (*purpose*)
S	**de manière que**	so that (*purpose*)
S	**de sorte que**	so that (in such a way that)
S	**de peur que**	for fear that
	depuis que	since (*time*)
S	**jusqu'à ce que**	until
	lorsque	when
	parce que	because
	pendant que	while
S	**pour que**	in order that
S	**pourvu que**	provided that
	puisque	since (because)
	quand	when
S	**sans que**	without

si if	
tandis que	while (whereas)
tant que	as long as
vu que	seeing that

It is important to remember that many of these words also exist in similar forms as prepositions [➤23]. The essential difference is that a preposition is followed by a noun or something that has the value of a noun, such as a pronoun or an infinitive; a subordinating conjunction is followed by a complete clause. The following examples illustrate the difference:

avant le repas	before the meal	(*preposition + noun*)
avant moi	before me	(*preposition + pronoun*)
avant de manger	before eating	(*preposition + infinitive*)
avant qu'ils mangent	before they eat	(*subordinating conjunction + subjunctive*)

[For more details on prepositions ➤23; on subjunctives ➤14; on negatives ➤25.]

5b Relative clauses

Relative clauses are introduced by relative pronouns [➤21j]. They describe or define a noun, and thus do the same job as an adjective [➤20]. The relative clause comes very soon (usually immediately) after the noun it refers to, for which reason the noun is known as the *antecedent*.

Les villes et les villages qu'ils traversent sont tous intéressants.	The towns and villages which they pass through are all interesting.

Here, **qu'ils traversent** is the relative clause describing **villes et villages**. It is vital to remember that in English, relative pronouns can take other forms (the towns and villages *that* they pass through) or be omitted altogether (the towns and villages they pass through), or provoke an alternative word order (through which they pass). This range of options is not generally available in French.

5c Direct and indirect speech

There are two ways of reporting what people have said (or perhaps thought). Both are introduced by verbs like **dire** (to say), and **répondre** (to answer).

(i) *Direct speech*

The first way is simply to repeat word for word what was said or thought. We call this *direct speech*, and in English it is marked by the use of quotation marks. Although the French punctuation is somewhat different [▶2c], the principle is similar to English:

¬J'ai une réunion à neuf heures et demie, dit-il.	"I have a meeting at half past nine," he said.
Je me suis dit: «Vous allez être en retard.»	I said to myself, "You're going to be late."

 Note from the above examples that phrases equivalent to "he said," "she replied," etc. in French have the word order inverted when they follow the direct speech (**dit-il**), but not when they introduce it (**Je me suis dit**).

(ii) *Indirect speech*

The second way is known as *indirect speech* or *reported speech*. What was said is rephrased, usually in a clause introduced by **que** or a question word:

Il a dit *qu'*il avait une réunion à neuf heures et demie.	He said (*that*) he had a meeting at half past nine.

You will see from the above example that in English the *that* which introduces indirect speech is often dropped.

(iii)

As you can see, direct speech is changed in several respects when it is reported in this way. Pronouns change (here from **je** to **il**). So do tenses, in many cases: **J'*ai* une réunion** becomes **il *avait* une réunion**.

The following table shows how tenses change from direct to indirect speech, when the speech is subsequently reported:

Direct speech	*Indirect speech*
present tense	imperfect tense
perfect tense	pluperfect tense
future tense	conditional tense

«Je travaille tard ce soir. J'ai commencé un rapport que je dois terminer. Je rentrerai sans doute vers minuit.»	"I am working late this evening. I've started a report that I have to finish. I'll no doubt be home about midnight."

becomes

Il a dit qu'il travaillait tard ce soir-là. Il avait commencé un rapport qu'il devait terminer. Il rentrerait sans doute vers minuit.	He said he was working late that evening. He had started a report that he had to finish. He would no doubt be home about midnight.

(iv)   The imperfect and conditional tenses in direct speech sometimes transfer unchanged into indirect speech:

«J'*irais* au cinéma si j'*avais* l'argent.»	"I *would go* to the movies if I *had* the money."
Il a dit qu'il *irait* au cinéma s'il *avait* l'argent.	He said he *would go* to the movies if he *had* the money.
«Je *serais allé* au cinéma si j'*avais eu* l'argent.»	"I *would have gone* to the movies if I *had had* the money."
Il a dit qu'il *serait allé* au cinéma s'il *avait eu* l'argent.	He said that he *would have gone* to the movies if he *had had* the money.

[For more on conditional tenses ➤12g.]

5d   *Indirect questions*

Indirect questions are a form of indirect speech [➤5c]. They obey the same rules and are introduced by the same types of verb, followed by the relevant question word. Indirect questions are used for various purposes:

(i)   To report a direct question that has been or will be asked

J'ai demandé où se trouvait l'hôtel Apollo.	I asked where the Apollo Hotel was situated.
Je demanderai où se trouve l'hôtel Apollo.	I'll ask where the Apollo Hotel is situated.

(ii) To ask more courteously (less direct generally equals more courteous!)

Pourriez-vous me dire si le concert a déjà commencé?	Could you tell me if the concert has already begun?

(iii) To say whether we know the answer to a question

Je ne sais pas pourquoi il n'a pas écrit.	I don't know why he hasn't written.

5e *Reported requests and commands*

These are usually dealt with in French by a construction with the infinitive:

Je lui ai dit de m'envoyer un chèque.	I told him to send me a check.

Asking for information: direct questions

6a   What is a direct question?

A direct question is a form of direct speech. It tells us word for word what the person said or thought. The questions in the examples below are all direct questions – these are the actual words used. [For indirect questions ➤5d.]

(i)   Information

At their simplest, questions are simply a matter of changing the intonation (the musical line) of the words, without any other changes:

–Je t'accompagne.	I'm going with you.

becomes

–Je t'accompagne?	Shall I go with you?

In the question the voice rises in note at the end of the utterance. This is a very common way of asking questions in speech, but is less appropriate in writing.

(ii)   Est-ce que...?

Equally common in everyday language – and perhaps the most widely accepted method of formulating questions – is simply to place **Est-ce que** in front of the statement:

–Est-ce que la circulation est très intense?	Is the traffic very heavy?
–Est-ce qu'ils connaissent la route?	Do they know the road?

Est-ce que is also frequently used in conjunction with other questioning words, in which case it follows the question word:

| –Quand est-ce que vous avez payé cette facture? | When did you pay this invoice? |
| –Pourquoi est-ce qu'il faut tout répéter trois fois? | Why do I have to repeat everything three times? |

(iii)   *Inversion*

Where a pronoun is the subject of the verb, questions can be formed by inverting the order of the subject and verb, inserting a hyphen. Although theoretically possible with all verbs, this method of forming questions is in everyday use limited to a range of common verbs, and in particular to verbs used as auxiliaries (**être**, **avoir**) and as modal verbs (**pouvoir**, **vouloir**, etc.) [➤9]:

–Peux-tu m'aider?	Can you help me?
–Sont-ils arrivés?	Have they arrived?
–Crois-tu qu'ils aient pu avoir des ennuis?	Do you think they might have gotten into difficulty?

(iv)   Where the subject is not a pronoun, questions can still be formed by inversion as in (iii) above, by the addition of a pronoun in the inverted position:

| –Les billets sont-ils arrivés? | Have the tickets arrived? |
| –Marie-Paule a-t-elle terminé son cours de piano? | Has Marie-Paule finished her piano lesson? |

(v)   *Question word +* ***est-ce que***

➤   Where question words like **Qui? Quand? Où?** and **Pourquoi?** are used, questions are formed either by adding **est-ce que** to the question word [➤6a (ii)], or by the use of inversion [➤6a (iii), (iv)]. For examples ➤6d. Note, however, that when **Qui? Quel?** [➤19b] and **Lequel?** [➤21g (v)] are used as subjects, they do not require an added inverted pronoun as in (iv) above:

| –Qui sont ces personnes? | Who are these people? |
| –Quelles sont les possibilités de paiement? | What are the possibilities for payment? |

–Laquelle serait la plus facile?	Which one would be the easiest?

6b   True or false? Yes-no questions

In this type of question we are asking whether something is true or not, so it is always possible to answer **oui** or **non**:

–Est-ce que tu vas en ville? –Oui.	"Are you going into town?" "Yes."
–Alors, tu peux m'emmener? –Non!	"Then can you give me a lift?" "No!"

6c   Checking up: tag questions

Tag questions are statements with a questioning tag added to the end to seek confirmation of the statement. English has an enormous number of tags such as *don't we? wouldn't you? isn't she?* though Americans use them less frequently, prefering *right?* and *OK?* In French however, there is one main question tag, **n'est-ce pas?**

–Nous pouvons partir ensemble, n'est-ce pas?	We can go together, can't we?
–Il y a de la place pour moi dans ta voiture, n'est-ce pas?	There's room for me in your car, isn't there?

Note that **n'est-ce pas?** is not used after negative questions. A general questioning expletive such as **hein?** may be used.

–Ils ne viennent pas ce soir, hein?	They are not coming this evening, are they?

Non is often used as a tag:

–Tu peux m'emmener, non?	You can take me with you, can't you?

6d   Asking for details: question-word questions

We use these questions when we want to find out more about something. They almost always start with a question-word, such as those listed below.

Many of the question words listed here are the same as or are closely related to other groups of words such as relative pronouns [➤21j]. Do not confuse them!

(i) *People:* ***Qui? Qui est-ce qui/que?*** *Who?*

[Interrogative pronouns ➤21g.]

–Qui va avec toi?	Who is going with you?
–Qui vas-tu rencontrer?/ Qui est-ce que tu vas rencontrer?	Who are you going to meet?

    –Avec qui...? A qui...? Pour qui...?, etc.

–Avec qui vas-tu manger?	Who are you eating with?
–A qui est ce manteau?	Whose is this coat?

(ii) *Things:* ***Qu'est-ce qui...? Qu'est-ce que...? Que...?*** *What?*

[Interrogative pronouns ➤21g.]

–Qu'est-ce qui t'inquiète?	What is worrying you?
–Qu'est-ce que tu vas faire en ville? Que vas-tu faire en ville?	What are you going to do in town?

(iii) *Selection*

–Quel chemin prends-tu?	Which road are you taking?

[Interrogative determiners ➤19a.]

–Lequel préfères-tu?	Which one do you prefer?

[Interrogative pronouns ➤21g.]

(iv) *Definition, description*

–Comment sont les petites routes?	What are the back roads like?
–Très enneigées.	Very snowbound.

PUTTING A SENTENCE TOGETHER

[For other uses of *comment* ➤(vii) below.]

(v)   Time

–Quand est-ce que tu pars?	When are you leaving?
–A quelle heure? Vers dix heures.	At what time? About ten.

(vi)   Place

–Où est ta voiture?	Where is your car?
–J'ai oublié.	I've forgotten.

(vii)   Manner, methods, and means

–Comment vas-tu la trouver, alors?	How are you going to find it then?

⚠ **Comment + être?** means *What is . . . like?*

–Comment est ta voiture?	What is your car like?
–Elle est rouge.	It's red.

Comment + **aller** means *How is/are . . .?* (asking after health, etc.).

–Comment va ton frère?	How is your brother?
–Il va mieux.	He's better.

You will see from the above examples that inversion after **Comment?** does not require an additional inverted pronoun, though this is perfectly possible as an alternative form:

–Ton frère, comment va-t-il?	How is your brother?

(viii)   Quantity and degree

(A) The question word for *How much?* and *How many?* in French is **Combien?** When used to ask about money, it often appears in fixed phrases such as:

–C'est combien?	How much is it?

When used to ask about numbers or quantities it is treated as an expression of quantity and is followed by **de**:

–Combien de glaçons veux-tu?	How many ice cubes would you like?
–Et combien d'eau?	And how much water?

(B) For questions about dimensions, height, length, age, size of clothes, and distance, the interrogative determiner **quel** [➤19a] is most often used:

–Quelle est la longueur de la pièce?	How long is the room?
–Tu prends quelle taille?	What size do you take? (*for clothes*)

 For shoes:

–Vous chaussez le combien?	What size shoes do you wear?

 Use **avoir** not **être** for age:

–Quel âge avez-vous?	How old are you?
–J'ai vingt-trois ans.	I'm twenty-three.

(C) For distances **à quelle distance** is used:

–Dijon est à quelle distance d'ici?	How far is Dijon from here?
–Au moins deux cent cinquante kilomètres.	At least two hundred and fifty kilometers

(D) For distances and times **à combien** is used:

–Paris est à combien d'ici?	How far is Paris from here?
–Deux heures par le train, trois heures en voiture.	Two hours by train, three by car.

(ix)   *Reasons:* ***Pourquoi?*** *Why?*

–**Pourquoi avez-vous choisi un appartement au 16e étage?**	Why did you choose an apartment on the 16th floor?
–**Pourquoi pas? Il y a un ascenseur.**	Why not? There is an elevator.

C
ACTIONS AND STATES:
VERBS AND THEIR USES

What verbs do

[For extensive treatment of the forms of French verbs, see the *Berlitz French Verb Handbook.*]

7a Actions, feelings, or states

Verbs are words that define *actions, feelings,* or *states:*

Je *voyage* beaucoup.	I *travel* a lot.
J'*aime* mon travail.	I *like* my work.
Je *suis* représentant.	I'*m* a salesman.

7b Simple and compound verbs

French verbs take simple tense forms, using single words as in the above examples, or *compound* forms made up with part of the verb **avoir** or the verb **être**:

J'*ai travaillé* toute ma vie dans l'électronique.	I *have worked* in electronics all my life.

Verbs may have a compound form in one language but not in another:

Je *suis devenu* représentant à l'âge de trente ans.	I *became* a salesman at the age of thirty.

7c Auxiliary verbs

When **avoir** and **être** are used in this way to create compound forms, they are known as *auxiliary verbs*, and are used in combination with a form of the main verb known as the *past participle* to produce a range of tenses [➤11b, 11c, 16]:

J'*aurais préféré* devenir médecin.	I *would have preferred* to become a doctor. (*perfect conditional*)
Si seulement j'*avais réussi mes examens.*	If only I *had passed* my exams. (*pluperfect*)
Je me *serais* sérieusement *avantagé.*	I *would have given* myself a real boost. (*perfect conditional*)

 Most verbs use **avoir** to form compound tenses. However, reflexive verbs [➤8c] and about a dozen other verbs [➤11c] form their compound tenses with **être**. In either case, the English equivalent does not vary:

J'ai fini.	I have finished.
Je me suis lavé.	I have washed (myself).
Je suis arrivé.	I have arrived.

The verb in the sentence

8a Subject and predicate

(i) All sentences must contain a subject and a predicate [➤4]. The predicate contains at least the main verb, but more often than not it adds other information.

Marie-Paule *sourit.*	Marie-Paule *smiles.* (*predicate consists of just the main verb*)
Elle *donne le journal à son mari.*	She *gives the newspaper to her husband.* (*predicate consists of main verb plus other information*)

(ii) *Transitive and intransitive verbs*

If, as in the first sentence above, no other information is necessary for the sentence to make sense, the verb is referred to as *intransitive*. In the second sentence, however, **Elle donne** makes incomplete sense without in this case a direct object, **le journal,** and an indirect object, **à son mari**. Verbs that need at least a direct object are known as *transitive*.

(iii) Some verbs can be used transitively or intransitively as needed:

L'horloge sonne.	The clock strikes. (*intransitive*)
L'horloge sonne l'heure.	The clock strikes the hour. (*transitive*)

(iv) The predicate of a sentence may contain many items of information besides those that are required to complete the sense of the main verb. The "optional extras" clarify or extend the meaning, but may be omitted without the sentence becoming nonsense:

Je préparais notre repas dans la cuisine vendredi soir vers huit heures.	I was preparing our meal in the kitchen on Friday evening about eight o'clock.

In the above example, the verb **préparais** requires a direct object, in this case **le repas**, to complete its sense, but the remainder of the sentence is grammatically optional, even though it may well contain important information.

 There is no guarantee that a verb which in French requires a direct object will necessarily do so in English [➤8b(ii)].

8b   *The direct object of transitive verbs*

(i)   Some verbs require a direct object in French, while others do not. Many more exist with or without a direct object, according to the context or meaning of the sentence.

J'utilise un stylo pour écrire.	I use a fountain pen for writing. (**Utiliser** *is always transitive; the direct object here is* **un stylo**.)
Je pars à huit heures.	I leave at eight o'clock (**Partir** *is always intransitive.*)
J'ai lu jusqu'à minuit.	I read until midnight. (**Lire** *used intransitively.*)
J'ai lu les dernières pages du roman.	I read the last pages of the novel. (**Lire** *used transitively; the direct object here is* **les dernières pages**.)

(ii)   A small number of verbs in French take a direct object where in English one would find an intransitive verb plus a preposition. The most common of these are:

attendre	wait for	**écouter**	listen to
chercher	look for	**habiter**	live in/at
demander	ask for	**regarder**	look at

J'attends le train de onze heures pour Orléans.	I'm waiting *for* the eleven o'clock train to Orléans.
J'habite un village tout près.	I live *in* a village nearby.
Je regarde ma montre. Il est onze heures moins cinq.	I look *at* my watch. It is five to eleven.

Je cherche le quai.	I look *for* the platform.
J'écoute les haut-parleurs sans	I listen *to* the loudspeakers without
rien comprendre.	understanding a word.
Je demande des	I ask *for* information at the ticket
renseignements au guichet.	window.

There are also many verbs that take a direct object in English but not in French [➤8d(ii)].

8c   Reflexive verbs

(i)   Turning the action back on the subject

A reflexive verb is a verb whose action is turned back on the subject. The object is therefore the same person or thing as the subject.

Il *se* pèse tous les jours.	He weighs *himself* every day.
Il *se* regarde dans la glace	He looks at *himself* in the mirror
et il *se* félicite d´être si beau.	and he congratulates *himself* on
	being so good-looking.

(ii)

In many cases reflexive verbs in French express an action whose reflexive nature is not stated (though it is perhaps understood) in English:

Je *me* lève à sept heures, je *me*	I get up at seven, wash, shave,
lave, je *me* rase, et je *m*'habille.	and get dressed.
Je *m*'entraîne deux fois par	I take the train twice a week.
semaine.	
Je *me* prépare rigoureusement	I prepare thoroughly for games . . .
pour les matchs...	
...et je *me* repose bien après.	. . . and I have a good rest afterward.

(iii)

In many cases the reflexive meaning is absent altogether from the English equivalent:

| Mes amis *se* moquent de moi... | My friends make fun of me . . . |

...mais ils ne *se* rendent pas compte des pressions de la vie sportive.	. . . but they don't realize the pressures of being in sports.

Other similar examples include:

s'adresser à	speak to	se moquer de	laugh at
s'en aller	go away	se noyer	drown
s'apercevoir de	notice	se plaindre	complain
s'approcher de	approach	se promener	go for a
se dépêcher	hurry		walk
se douter de	suspect	se souvenir de	remember
se fier à	trust	se servir de	use
s'imaginer	imagine	se rendre à	go to
se méfier de	mistrust	se taire	shut up,
se mettre à	begin to		be silent

(iv) Actions done to each other

Verbs can be used in the reflexive form to express actions done *to each other.*

Ils *se* voient toutes les semaines, ils *se* téléphonent, et ils *s'*écrivent.	They see *each other* every week, they telephone (*each other*), and they write (*to each other*).

(v) Reflexive instead of English passive

Reflexive verb forms are frequently used where a passive form would be used in English [➤15c].

Les champs de tournesols *se* voient partout maintenant.	Fields of sunflowers are to be seen everywhere nowadays.

(vi)

Reflexive verbs often convey the idea of "becoming," as in verbs like these:

se fâcher	get angry	se refroidir	cool down,
s'énerver	get annoyed		get cold
se fatiguer	get tired	se soûler	get drunk
se réchauffer	get warm	s'enrhumer	catch a cold

➤ [For a full list of reflexive pronouns ➤21b(vi).
For the position of the reflexive pronouns ➤21b(vii), (viii).
For the use of auxiliaries in compound tenses ➤11c.]

8d   Direct or indirect objects

(i)   A process of transfer: verbs with two objects

Some transitive verbs describe a process of transfer between people, for example, verbs such as **donner** (to give), **envoyer** (to send) and **parler** (to speak). These verbs have two objects – the direct object and the indirect object (the person or thing to which the process is applied):

Le moniteur donne les skis à Patrick.	The instructor gives the skis to Patrick.

Les skis are the direct object; **Patrick** is the indirect object.

In French, as the above example shows, the indirect object is introduced by the preposition **à**, which can of course exist also in forms such as **au, à la, aux** [➤19c] or be replaced by a pronoun [➤21b(v)], as in this example:

Le moniteur lui passe les skis.	The instructor passes the skis to him.

Lui = à Patrick

In English the preposition is often required, as in: "The instructor gives Patrick the skis." and "The instructor passes him the skis." In French no such option exists. English speakers need to be very careful about this. A similar danger exists for English speakers when expressing passive constructions. In French, the indirect object cannot become the subject of a passive construction as in the English "Patrick is given the skis."

In French this idea would have to be expressed:

On donne les skis à Patrick.	Patrick is given the skis. (One gives the skis to Patrick.)

[For more details of passive forms and equivalents ➤15c.]

(ii)   Some verbs in French take an indirect object where the English equivalent has a direct object. The most common are:

obéir à (*also* désobéir)	
Il obéit toujours à son père.	He always obeys his father.
pardonner à	
Est-ce qu'elle pardonnera à sa mère de l'avoir abondonnée?	Will she forgive her mother for abandoning her?
plaire à (*also* déplaire)	
C'est un cadeau qui plaira beaucoup aux enfants.	It's a present that will greatly please the children.
succéder à	
Qui va succéder au directeur actuel?	Who is going to succeed the present (company) director?
Survivre à	
Voilà un cas où la mère a survécu à ses enfants.	This is a case where the mother has survived her children.
téléphoner à	
As-tu téléphoné à la police?	Have you telephoned the police?

(iii)   *Doing something for someone*

The indirect object form (generally in this case a personal pronoun) is also commonly used in speech to express the idea of doing something *for* someone:

Est-ce que tu peux *m'*emmener ces lettres à la poste et *m'*acheter des timbres en même temps?	Can you take these letters to the post office *for me* and buy *(for)* me some stamps at the same time?

8e   *Verbs + preposition + noun*

(i)   The addition of prepositions (most often **à** or **de**) to link a verb to its object is a common feature of the French language. The following checklist brings together the verbs most likely to cause difficulty to English speakers, either because in English a preposition would not be required or because the preposition would be different.

acheter à	buy from	**s'apercevoir de**	notice
		(*but* **apercevoir**	catch sight of)

VERBS

arracher à	snatch, tear away from	se mêler à	get involved in
s'approcher de	approach, draw near	nuire à	harm
		obéir à,	obey,
assister à	be present at	désobéir à	disobey
(but assister)	assist	pardonner à	forgive
avoir besoin de	need	penser de/à	think of (opinion), think about
changer de	change		
convenir à	suit	plaire à,	please,
croire à/en	believe something/ believe in	déplaire à	displease
		punir de	punish for
		récompenser de	reward for
dépendre de	depend on	réfléchir à	reflect on
(se) douter de	doubt	remercier de	thank for
s'emparer de	grab	renoncer à	give up
emprunter à	borrow from	résister à	resist
entrer dans	enter	ressembler à	resemble, look alike
féliciter de	congratulate on		
se fier à	trust	(se) servir de/à	put to use as/to be used for
s'intéresser à	be interested in		
jouer de/à	play (an instrument/ a game)	se souvenir de	remember
		succéder à	succeed
		survivre à	survive
		téléphoner à	telephone
jouir de	enjoy	se tromper de	mistake
manquer de/à	lack/fail in	vivre de	live on
se méfier de	mistrust	voler à	steal from

(ii) Verbs using different prepositions to give different meanings

croire à	believe something (to be true)
croire en	be a believer

Je crois à son honnêteté.	I believe in his honesty.
Je crois en Dieu.	I believe in God.

jouer de	play (a musical instrument)
jouer à	play (a game or sport)

Elle joue du clavecin.	She plays the harpsichord.
Elle joue aussi au rugby.	She also plays football.

manquer	miss
manquer de	lack, be short of
manquer à	fail in

Il a manqué son train.	He has missed his train.
Elle manque de discrétion.	She lacks tact.
Nous avons manqué à nos	We have failed in our
responsabilités.	responsabilities.

Note also the useful expression **tu me manques** "I miss you," **Est-ce que je t'ai manqué?** "Did you miss me?"

| penser de | think of (have an opinion about) |
| penser à | think of (direct one's thoughts to) |

Que pensez-vous de notre	What do you think of our new
nouveau collègue?	colleague?
Je pense souvent à ma jeunesse.	I often think of my youth.
Pensez à moi!	Think of me!

servir	serve (for example, in a restaurant)
servir à	be used/useful for
servir de	put to use as
se servir de	use

Il m'a servi une bière.	He served me a beer.
A quoi sert cet appareil?	What is this machine used for?
Le sol va servir de table.	The ground will do as a table.
Je me sers toujours d'un	I always use a screwdriver to open
tournevis pour ouvrir une boîte	a can of paint.
de peinture.	

8f *Verbs followed by infinitives*

In English, verbs are mostly linked to following infinitives by the preposition *to* ("I prefer *to* stay in bed"). In a few cases, no linking preposition is required ("I must stay in bed, I cannot go out"). French is similar, except that there are three possibilities:

Je demande *à* rester au lit.	I ask *to* stay in bed.
Je refuse *de* rester au lit.	I refuse *to* stay in bed.
Je préfère rester au lit.	I prefer *to* stay in bed.

41

Each verb linked to an infinitive in this way has its own perma-nent pairing with either **à**, **de**, or a *bare infinitive.*

It is also very common in English to use the present participle instead of this infinitive ("I like *staying* in bed"). This construction does not exist in French. An infinitive construction must be used [➤8(i)].

(i) *Verbs + bare infinitive*

A small number of verbs are linked to a following infinitive with-out any preposition. They include:

(A) Modal verbs: **pouvoir, vouloir, devoir, falloir, savoir** [➤9].

Je *voudrais* aller avec toi, mais je ne *peux* pas sortir, je *dois* être là quand les enfants reviendront de l'école.	I *would like* to go with you, but I *can't* go out, I *have to* be here when the children come home from school.

(B) Verbs expressing like, dislike, preference, hope, expecta-tion, and wishes:

adorer	adore, love	**détester**	hate
aimer	like	**espérer**	hope
compter	expect	**préférer**	prefer
désirer	want, wish	**souhaiter**	wish

Je *déteste* conduire quand il y a du brouillard; il vaut mieux laisser la voiture au garage ces jours-là. Je *préfère* sortir en voiture quand il fait beau. Je *compte* pouvoir le faire en Italie l'été prochain. J'*adore* rouler le toit ouvert.	I *hate* driving when it's foggy; it's better to leave the car in the garage on those days. I *prefer* to go out in the car when it's fine and sunny. I *expect* to be able to do that in Italy next summer. I *love* driving with the sunroof open.

The infinitive construction illustrated above after verbs expressing wish is possible only when the verb and the infinitive have the same subject. The verb + infinitive construction cannot be used in French to convey English sentences of the type "want/prefer *him* to drive." To express this idea in French, one must use a separate clause [➤14].

(C) Verbs of motion:

aller	go	**monter**	come/go up
courir	run	**partir**	leave
descendre	come/go down	**rentrer**	come/go back
entrer	enter	**sortir**	leave/go out
envoyer	send	**venir**	come

Il est sorti faire ses courses.	He has gone out to do his shopping.

Some of the above are used in expressions that would be equivalent to the English "Go and . . .", or "Run and . . . ."

Je suis descendu prendre du vin à la cave.	I went down *and* fetched (to fetch) some wine from the cellar.

(D) Verbs of seeing, hearing, and feeling:

écouter	listen to	**regarder**	watch
entendre	hear	**(se) sentir**	feel
voir	see		

Je l'ai vu passer, puis je l'ai entendu crier.	I saw him go past, then I heard him cry out.

(E) The verbs **sembler**, **laisser**, and **faire**:

Je l'ai fait rentrer. Il semblait vouloir dire quelque chose. Je l'ai laissé parler.	I let him in. He seemed to want to say something. I let him speak.

➤ [For a more detailed treatment of *faire* and *laisser* ➤9f].

(ii) *Verbs + à + infinitive*

This is a small group of fairly common verbs. The use of **à** generally signals intention, aim, or direction:

s'amuser à	enjoy oneself (doing . . .)
apprendre à	learn to, teach how to . . .
s'apprêter à	get ready to . . .
arriver à	manage to . . .
avoir à	have to . . .

VERBS

chercher à	seek to . . .
commencer à	start to . . . , begin (doing . . .)
consentir à	agree to . . .
continuer à	carry on (doing . . .)
se décider à	make up one's mind to . . .
(*but* **décider de**)	decide to
demander à	ask to . . .
encourager à	encourage to . . .
s'habituer à	get used to (doing . . .)
hésiter à	hesitate to . . .
s'intéresser à	be interested in (doing . . .)
inviter à	invite to . . .
se mettre à	begin to . . .
obliger à	oblige to . . .
passer du temps à	spend time (doing . . .)
perdre du temps à	waste time (doing . . .)
persister à	persist in (doing . . .)
pousser à	urge to . . .
renoncer à	give up (doing . . .)
réussir à	succeed in (doing . . .)
servir à	be used for (doing . . .)
tarder à	delay, be late (doing . . .)
tenir à	be eager to . . .

(iii) *verbs + de + infinitive*

Most verb + infinitive constructions in French belong to this group. If a verb is not to be found in the two groups above [➤8f(i), (ii)], it is likely that it uses **de** to link with its infinitive, for example:

Il refuse *de* m'accompagner.	He refuses to go with me.
Il m'accuse *d'*avoir organisé la réunion sans le consulter. J'ai essayé *de* le dissuader et je l'ai remercié *de* m'avoir aidé jusqu'à présent. Je ne sais pas quoi faire.	He accuses me of having organized the meeting without consulting him. I have tried to dissuade him and I've thanked him for helping me up to now. I don't know what to do.

8g *Verbs + present participle*

This is a very common construction in English (he enjoys swimming, she likes riding), but there is no equivalent use of the present participle in French. Instead the verb in French is followed by an infinitive [➤8f].

8h *Verbs + past participle*

The verbs that most frequently combine with past participles in French are **avoir** and **être** when used as auxiliaries to form compound tenses [➤11c].

The verb **être** is also used with past participles to form passive constructions, such as:

Le restaurant est géré par un de mes amis.	The restaurant is run by a friend of mine.

[To express in French the idea conveyed by the English expression, "to have/get something done," ➤9f.]

Attitudes to action: modal verbs

A modal verb seldom carries a full meaning by itself. Instead, as the list below shows, a modal verb says something about the relationship between the subject and the full verb, which is in the infinitive. It creates a *mood* for the verb that follows:

Je *dois* voir un médecin.	I *must* see a doctor.
Pouvez-vous m'aider?	*Can* you help me?

The modal verbs in French are:

devoir	have to, must	**savoir**	know how to
falloir	be necessary	**vouloir**	wish
pouvoir	be able, can		

The precise use and variations of meaning of the modal verbs are explained in the following sections.

9a Devoir

The verb **devoir** expresses obligation, adding nuance and variation to this central meaning by the use of different tenses. It corresponds to a range of English equivalents, from the direct *I must*, I *have to*, through to *I should*, *I ought*, *I ought to have.* It is also used (as in English) to express strong supposition such as "The parcel must have arrived."

(i) *In the present tense*

As the most *immediate* tense, the present tense of **devoir** expresses the strongest meaning.

Elle *doit* m'obéir.	She *must* obey me.
Je *dois* aller au Maroc la semaine prochaine.	I *have to* go to Morocco next week.

It also expresses strong supposition, especially (though not exclusively) when used as an impersonal verb.

| Il *doit* faire chaud au Maroc en ce moment. | It *must* be hot in Morocco at the moment. |
| Vous *devez* être content d'aller dans un pays chaud. | You *must* be pleased to be going to a hot country. |

(ii)   *In the perfect tense*

| Ma femme *a dû* partir avant moi. | My wife *has had* to leave before me. (*obligation*) My wife *had* to leave before me. (*obligation*) My wife *must have* left before me. (*supposition*) |

(iii)   *In the imperfect tense*

| Ma feme *devait* partir avant moi. | My wife *was going to have* to leave before me. (*obligation*) My wife was supposed to leave before me. (*supposition*) |

(iv)   *In the pluperfect tense*

| Ma femme *avait dû* partir avant moi. | My wife *had* to leave before me. |

(v)   *In the conditional*

The conditional provides a widely used form of **devoir**, equivalent to the English "ought" or "should."

| Je *devrais* lui téléphoner. | I *ought* to telephone her. (*obligation*) I *should* telephone her. |

On occasions it means "would have to," but this idea is more frequently expressed by using **obliger**:

| Si je n'obtenais pas de visa, elle *serait obligée* de rentrer. | If I didn't get a visa, she *would have* to come back. |

(vi) *In the conditional perfect*

The conditional perfect is widely used to convey the equivalent of the English "ought to have" or "should have."

J'*aurais dû* lui téléphoner ce matin.	I *should have* telephoned her this morning. (*obligation*) I *ought to* have telephoned her this morning.

It is occasionally used to convey "would have had to."

Si je n'avais pas obtenu mon visa, j'*aurais dû* abandonner le projet.	If I hadn't gotten a visa, I *would have had* to abandon the project.

Devoir also exists as an ordinary nonmodal verb, with the meaning "to owe."

Ma banque me *doit* deux cents francs.	My bank *owes* me two hundred francs.

9b   Falloir

(i) *Necessity or obligation*

The verb **falloir** exists only in the impersonal form **il faut** and its other tenses. Like **devoir**, it conveys the idea of necessity or obligation, but its impersonal form means that the necessity can be expressed without stating on whom the obligation falls:

Il faut trouver une solution.	A solution has to be found.

(ii) *Present tense*

Even though this is an impersonal verb, the context will often mean that it is interpreted more personally:

Il *faut* surtout lui demander de nous rembourser.	*We must* certainly ask him for our money back.

Theoretically, **il faut** can be personalized by the use of the indirect object pronoun:

Il me faut partir.	*I must* go.

However, this particular construction is now considered old-fashioned and stiff, and instead one says:

Il faut que je parte.	*I must* go.

This uses the subjunctive [➤14], which, contrary to the widely held prejudice among English-speaking learners of French, is commonly used.

(iii) Other tenses

Il faut exists in other tenses, with meanings similar to those for **devoir** [➤9a]:

Il fallait que je parte très tôt.	*I had* to leave very early./*It was necessary* for me to leave very early. (*imperfect*)
Il faudrait partir tout de suite.	*We/You/I ought* to leave right away. (*conditional*)

Note in the first of the above examples that the subjunctive **je parte** is in the present tense, even though the main verb **il fallait** is in the imperfect tense. The present tense of the subjunctive is the only tense in everyday use [➤17f].

9c Pouvoir

(i) Being able to

Pouvoir expresses the idea of "being able to," "being physically capable of," "being allowed to," "having permission to," and has a variety of equivalents in English, such as "can," "could," "may" and "might."

Je *peux* **stationner là?**	*Can* I/*May* I park here? (Do I have permission?)
Je *ne peux pas* **ouvrir la porte.**	*I can't* open the door. (*incapable*)

Nous *pouvons* passer la journée ensemble.	We *can* spend the day together.

(ii)   *Possibility*

Pouvoir also expresses possibility, especially when used in the conditional tense:

Elle *pourrait* arriver ce soir, mais cela m'étonnerait.	She *could* arrive this evening, but I would be very surprised.
Elle *aurait pu* manquer le train.	She *could have* missed the train.

(iii)   *Se pouvoir*

Possibility can also be expressed by using the impersonal reflexive form **se pouvoir:**

Il *se peut* que quelqu'un l'ait vue.	*It's possible* someone may have seen her.

Note that **se pouvoir** is followed by a subjunctive [➤14c].

(iv)   **Pouvoir** can be used in conjunction with the infinitive of impersonal forms such as **il y a** (infinitive **y avoir**) or **il arrive**:

Il *peut y avoir* un problème.	*There may be* a problem.
Il *pourrait arriver* que...	*It could happen* that . . .

9d   Savoir

(i)   *Savoir vs. pouvoir*

Savoir has only limited use as a modal verb, with the meaning "to know how to." However, since this idea is frequently expressed in English by the word "can," there is a danger that English speakers will confuse the use of **savoir** and **pouvoir**.

Tu *peux* conduire, si tu veux.	You *can* drive, if you like.
Non, je *ne peux pas*, je *ne sais pas* conduire.	No, I *can't.* I *can't* drive.

(ii) **Je ne saurais pas**

The expression **Je ne saurais pas** is used to convey "I could not possibly," "I could not bring myself to."

Je ne saurais pas **abandonner mes enfants.**	*I couldn't possibly* abandon my children.

(iii) **Savoir**, *"to know"*

Savoir is much more common as a nonmodal verb, meaning "to know."

Savez-vous **à quel étage ils habitent?**	*Do you know* what floor they live on?
Non, mais je *sais* **que ce n'est pas au rez-de-chaussée.**	No, but I *know* it's not on the ground floor.

9e **Vouloir**

(i) *Expressing wish*

As with other modal verbs [➤9a-d], **vouloir** has a variety of equivalents in English. It is the basic verb in French for expressing wish:

Je *veux* **m'acheter un nouveau costume.**	I *want* to buy myself a new suit.
Elle ne *veut* **pas divorcer.**	She doesn't *want* a divorce.

(ii) *Expressing willingness*

Vouloir is also widely used to express willingness, particularly in set expressions such as **Je veux bien**, "I am willing."

Je veux bien **l'aider, mais il ne veut pas.**	*I'm willing* to help him, but he refuses.

Voulez-vous, and **Veux-tu** are standard formulations for polite requests:

Voulez-vous **me suivre, s'il vous plaît?**	*Will you* follow me, please?
Veux-tu **un chocolat?**	*Would you like* a chocolate?

(iii)   *Should like...*

Conditional forms of **vouloir** are also commonly used to express "should like," and "should have liked."

Je *voudrais* **un kilo de pommes.**	I *should like* a kilo of apples.
J'*aurais voulu* **le remercier.**	I *should have liked* to thank him.

  In English it is customary to use a conditional for polite requests "Would you like," "Would you mind." In this instance the French equivalent tends to be the simple present tense form. This explains why French people speaking English sometimes say 'Do you want a chocolate?" when their intention is to say "Would you like," an error that can give a wholly undeserved impression of brusqueness.

Note   **Vouloir** is used in the expression **en vouloir à quelqu'un,** meaning "to bear someone a grudge":

Il *m'en veut* **parce que j'ai eu une augmentation.**	He *has a grudge against me* because I got a pay raise.

➤   [For the use of *vouloir* as an imperative ➤13b(iii).]

9f   Faire, laisser, *etc.* + *infinitive*

The verbs covered in this section are not modal verbs [➤9a–e], but can be used with infinitives in similar ways, to create new or modified meanings.

(i)   *Faire*

(A) Faire + infinitive means "to have something done" or "get something done."

Est-ce que le propriétaire *a fait réparer* **la voiture?**	Has the owner *had* the car *repaired*?

Oui, il l'*a fait réparer*.	Yes, he *has had* it *repaired*.

 With **faire** + infinitive constructions, any object pronoun (**l'** in the above example) is placed before *both* verbs, not before the infinitive as in the majority of verb + infinitive forms. Note also that when the past participle **fait** is used, as here, it does not follow the normal pattern of agreeing with the preceding direct object [➤10c].

(B) Faire + inifinitive also means "to get someone to do something."

L'instituteur *a fait chanter sa classe*.	The teacher *got his class to sing*.

Notice that the word order is different in English: in French **sa classe** cannot be placed between **fait** and **chanter**.

If **faire** + infinitive is followed by two objects, the one relating to **faire** has to be made an indirect object:

L'instituteur a fait chanter la Marseillaise *à sa classe*.	The teacher got *his class* to sing the Marseillaise.

(C) Faire + reflexive verb in infinitive: if the infinitive following **faire** is reflexive, the reflexive pronoun is omitted:

L'instituteur fait asseoir sa classe.	The teacher gets his class to sit down.

 To express "to make someone do something" do not use **faire**; use a verb such as **obliger**.

Il les *oblige* à s'asseoir.	He *makes* them sit down.

(D) Note also:

faire voir	show

Il m'*a fait voir* ses photos.	He *showed* me his photos.

faire entrer	show (someone) in	**faire venir**	send for
faire sortir	show (someone) out		

(ii)   Laisser

With a following infinitive, **laisser** means "to let someone do something," or "to let something happen."

Il *nous a laissé sortir* par la porte arrière.	He *let us out* by the back door.

• The special rules relating to past participle agreements and to reflexive verbs when **faire** is used with an infinitive [➤9f(i) above] also apply to **laisser** when used in this way.

• Note the frequently found **laisser tomber**, "to drop." This is used particularly in the sense of dropping a subject or proposal. It should not be confused with **faire tomber**, "to drop or knock over" an object.

⟦10⟧ Verb forms not related to time

10a The infinitive

The infinitive is the part of the verb most commonly listed in dictionaries. It is the verb's "title" - it names a certain action or state without relating it to a particular occasion. When used in a sentence, it behaves more like a noun, for example, following a main verb or a preposition:

Je préfère *rester*.	I prefer *to stay*.
Elle aimerait *partir*.	She would like *to leave*.

(i) Types of infinitive

Infinitives of most verbs in French end in **-er**, **-ir**, or **-re**. A small number end in **-oir**.

fumer	to smoke	**vendre**	to sell
finir	to finish	**recevoir**	to receive

(ii) Uses

The main uses of the infinitive are described in these paragraphs.

➤ [For *bare* infinitives ➤8f(i); verbs + prepositions + infinitives ➤8f(ii), (iii); modal verbs + infinitives ➤9.]

(iii) Infinitives as nouns

Having the value of a noun, an infinitive can serve, for example, as subject or object of a verb:

***Voyager* coûte cher.**	*Traveling* is expensive.
Mais j'adore *voir* d'autres pays.	But I love *seeing* other countries.

 It is important to remember that in English the verb form *-ing* is often used where the French use the infinitive. The examples above illustrate this.

(iv)   *Negative infinitives*

When an infinitive is made negative, the **ne** and **pas** that normally surround the verb are placed together before the infinitive [➤25b]:

Ce serait dommage de *ne pas visiter* d'autres pays.	*Not to visit* other countries would be a shame.

(v)   Some infinitives have taken on a distinct identity as nouns in their own right, such as:

le devoir	duty	**le rire**	laughter
le savoir	knowledge		

10b   *The present participle*

(i)   *Formation*

The present participle in French is formed by removing the **-ons** ending from the first person plural of the present tense and then adding **-ant**.

nous partons	→	**partant**	leaving
nous finissons	→	**finissant**	finishing

The only exceptions are **ayant** (**avoir**), **étant** (**être**), and **sachant** (**savoir**).

Negative forms are as for simple verbs:

***N'ayant pas* de leurs nouvelles, je leur ai écrit.**	*Not having* heard from them, I wrote to them.

 The English form in *-ing* is much more widely used than the present participle in French. [➤10b(iii) for a list of traps when translating from English.]

(ii)   *Use of the present participle as an adjective*

When used as an adjective, the present participle agrees with the noun in the normal way:

une étoile filant*e*	a shooting star
des scènes effrayant*es*	frightening scenes

(iii)   Use of the present participle as a verb

(A) When used as a verb, the present participle in French is frequently preceded by **en**, to give the meaning "on," "by," or "while."

En arrivant à la maison j'ai téléphoné au garage.	On arriving home I phoned the garage.
J'ai trouvé le numéro en regardant dans l'annuaire.	I found the number by looking in the telephone book.
En attendant que le garage réponde, j'ai remarqué une enveloppe sur la tablette.	While waiting for the garage to answer, I noticed an envelope on the small table.

(B) The use of **tout** before **en** adds emphasis to the fact of two simultaneous actions or introduces a concession in an argument:

Tout en conduisant, il a enlevé sa veste.	While still driving the car, he took off his jacket.
Tout en acceptant que tu as droit à tes opinions, je ne vais pas changer d'avis.	While I accept that you have a right to your opinions, I'm not going to change my mind.

(C) When the present participle is used without **en**, the actions described follow one after the other.

Ramassant ses bagages, il est sorti sans dire un mot.	Picking up his luggage, he left without saying a word.

(iv)   Translating the English -ing

The English -ing is not equivalent to the French **-ant** in the following cases:

• When -ing forms part of a tense in English:

je vais	I am going	**j'attendais**	I was waiting

• After prepositions:

sans attendre	without waiting

• when linked to a preceding verb:

J'aime danser.	I like dancing.
Il évite de parler anglais.	He avoids speaking English.
Elle se met à pleurer.	She starts crying.

(v) Present participle as a noun

The present participle is sometimes used as a noun, for example, **un(e) passant(e)** (a passerby), **un(e) survivant(e)** (a survivor).

Note, however, that many -ing nouns in English have equivalents in French that are not connected with the past participle, for example:

la natation	swimming	**la chasse**	hunting
l'équitation	horseback riding	**la pêche**	fishing
le jardinage	gardening	**le traitement**	word
la danse	dancing	**de texte**	processing

10c The past participle

(i) Formation

The past participle of regular verbs is formed as follows:

infinitive	*past participle*
porter	porté
finir	fini
vendre	vendu

[For the past participle of irregular verbs ➤17f.]

(ii) The uses of the past participle

(A) In the formation of compound tenses:

J'ai *suivi* vos instructions.	I *followed* your instructions.
Je suis *allé* au bureau du service après-vente.	I *went* to the customer service office.

[For full details on the use of the past participle in compound tenses ➤11, 12.]

(B) With **être** to form the passive:

La visite *est suivie* d'un repas.	The visit *is followed* by a meal.

[For full details on the use of the past participle to form passives ➤15.]

(C) As an adjective, in which case it agrees with the noun in the usual way:

Fatigués et *déçus*, ils sont rentrés chez eux.	*Tired* and *disappointed*, they returned to their homes.

 The *past* participle is sometimes used in French, where the *present* participle is used in English particularly when describing positions.

assis	sitting	**appuyé**	leaning
couché	lying	**agenouillé**	kneeling
penché	bending over	**(sus)pendu**	hanging

Je suis suspendu à tes lèvres.	I am hanging on your every word (literally, "on your lips").

11 The passage of time and tenses

11a   What do tenses tell us?

Tense is not the same thing as time, though the same words are often used to refer to both. Time is a fact of life, in which there are only three time zones (past, present, and future). Tenses, on the other hand, are grammatical structures that often reflect a way of looking at an event as well as just recording when it happened. The number of tenses, the names given to them, and their uses vary greatly from one language to another.

11b   One word or two? Simple and compound tenses

In the language of grammar a *simple* tense is a one-word form, while a *compound* tense uses two or more words (an auxiliary verb + one or more participles). In the indicative mood, French has five simple tenses and five compound tenses; in the subjunctive mood, it has two simple tenses and two compound tenses.

[For a definition of (indicative and subjunctive) *mood* ➤14a.]

11c   Which tenses do I need to learn?

If the prospect of learning seven simple and seven compound tenses is a daunting one, you should bear in mind that not all learners of French will need all these tenses. Some tenses are used only in the written language and in formal registers. You may choose to avoid learning these altogether, or simply learn to recognize them, for use when reading. Spend a few moments studying the following checklist, which gives a rating for each tense in terms of its usefulness in the spoken and written language (●●● very useful, ●● useful, ● rarely needed). Where a tense is not used in speech, this is indicated as ×××.

Simple tenses		*Speech*	*Written*
Present	**je mange**	●●●	●●●
	I eat, do eat, am eating		
Future	**je mangerai**	●●	●●●
	I shall eat		

Imperfect	**je mangeais** *I was eating, used to eat*	●●●	●●●
Conditional	**je mangerais** *I would eat*	●●●	●●●
Past historic	**je mangeai** *I ate*	×××	●●
Present subjunctive	**je mange** *I eat*	●●●	●●●
Imperfect subjunctive	**Je mangeasse** *I ate*	×××	●

Compound tenses		*Speech*	*Written*
Perfect	**j'ai mangé** *I have eaten, I ate*	●●●	●●●
Pluperfect	**j'avais mangé** *I had eaten*	●●●	●●●
Future perfect	**j'aurai mangé** *I shall have eaten*	●	●●●
Conditional perfect	**j'aurais mangé** *I would have eaten*	●●	●●●
Past anterior	**j'eus mangé** *I had eaten*	×××	●
Perfect subjunctive	**j'aie mangé** *I have eaten*	●●	●●
Pluperfect subjunctive	**j'eusse mangé** *I had eaten*	×××	●

11d   Auxiliary verbs used to form compound tenses

(i)   Avoir

Most verbs in French form their compound tenses using **avoir** as the auxiliary:

Perfect infinitive	**avoir mangé**	to have eaten
Perfect	**j'ai mangé**	I have eaten, I ate
Pluperfect	**j'avais mangé**	I had eaten
Future perfect	**j'aurai mangé**	I shall have eaten
Conditional perfect	**j'aurais mangé**	I should have eaten
Past anterior	**j'eus mangé**	I had eaten
Perfect subjunctive	**que j'aie mangé**	I have eaten, I ate
Pluperfect subjunctive	**que j'eusse mangé**	I had eaten

61

(ii) Être

A small number of verbs form their compound tenses with **être**:

Perfect infinitive	**être arrivé**	to have arrived
Perfect	**je suis arrivé**	I have arrived, I arrived
Pluperfect	**j'étais arrivé**	I had arrived
Future perfect	**je serai arrivé**	I shall have arrived
Conditional perfect	**je serais arrivé**	I should have arrived
Past anterior	**je fus arrivé**	I had arrived
Perfect subjunctive	**que je sois arrivé**	I have arrived, I arrived
Pluperfect subjunctive	**que je fusse arrivé**	I had arrived

All reflexive verbs and the following verbs and verbs based on them form their compound tenses with **être**.

aller	go
venir (+ **devenir**, **revenir**, **parvenir**, etc.)	come (become, come back, arrive, etc.)
retourner	go back
arriver	arrive
partir (+ **repartir**)	leave
entrer (+ **rentrer**)	go/come in
sortir (+ **ressortir**)	go/come out
monter (+ **remonter**)	go/come up
descendre (+ **redescendre**)	go/come down
tomber (+ **retomber**)	fall
naître (+ **renaître**)	be born
mourir	die
rester	remain

(iii) Reflexive verbs

Many verbs exist both in reflexive and nonreflexive forms. They take **être** when reflexive, **avoir** otherwise:

Je me suis lavé.	I washed myself.
J'ai lavé la voiture.	I washed the car.

Note also that the verbs in (ii) above take **être** only when used intransitively, that is, without an object [➤8a]. A few verbs in the list can also be used transitively, that is, with an object. When this happens, they take **avoir** in compound forms:

Elle est sortie à midi.	She went out at noon.
Elle a sorti la voiture.	She took the car out.
Je suis descendu.	I went downstairs.
J'ai descendu les bagages.	I took the luggage downstairs.

11e *Past participle agreement in compound tenses*

The following rules for agreement of past participles apply across all compound tenses.

(i) *Compounds formed with* **avoir**

Normally the past participle of a verb conjugated with **avoir** remains unchanged:

Elle a *perdu* ses lunettes de soleil.	She has *lost* her sunglasses.

However, if the verb has a direct object, *and the direct object precedes the verb*, the past participle agrees with the number and gender of the direct object. In the above example, the direct object *follows* the verb (as it most frequently does), and no agreement is required. The examples below show how the direct object can precede the verb:

When the direct object is a relative pronoun [➤21j]:

Voilà les lunettes que j'avais *perdues*.	Here are the glasses that I had lost. (*direct object is* **que**, which refers back to **les lunettes**)

When the direct object is an object pronoun [➤21b(vi)]:

Je les ai *perdues* dans le sable.	I lost them in the sand. (*direct object* **les** – i.e., **les lunettes** – normally precedes verb)

When the direct object is an interrogative determiner [➤21g, 19b]:

| Lesquelles as-tu *perdues*, les vieilles? | Which ones did you lose, the old ones? (*direct object is* **lesquelles**, i.e., **les lunettes**) |

(ii) Compounds formed with être

A small group of verbs [➤11c] form their compound tenses with **être**. The past participles of these verbs agree in number and gender with the subject of the verb:

| Nous sommes *allés* au match ensemble mais elle est *rentrée* avant moi. | We *went* to the game together but she *came back* before me. |

Since most reflexive verbs have a direct object (the reflexive pronoun) that precedes the verb, the past participle agrees, following the pattern outlined in (i) above.

| Elle s'est *couchée* à minuit. | She went to bed at midnight. |

 With some reflexive verbs the reflexive pronoun is an *indirect object,* in which case there is no past participle agreement:

| Ils se sont *téléphoné* tous les jours. | They *phoned* (to) each other every day. |
| Elle s'est *frotté* les yeux. | She *rubbed* her eyes. (she rubbed the eyes to herself) |

The use of tenses

One of the principal differences between tenses in French and in English is that each French tense has only one form, whereas in English there are several variations on the wording of many tenses.

In this section we consider the use of the range of French tenses in the *indicative mood*. The indicative mood is the standard use of the verb, to be contrasted with the *subjunctive mood* (which generally introduces an element of conjecture, purpose, wish, fear, etc., ➤14) or the *imperative mood* (which relates to commands ➤13).

12a   *The present tense*

(i)   In French, each verb has only one present tense form:

je marche, tu marches, etc.

[For details of the formation of the present tense ➤16b.]

This single verb form covers several alternative forms in English:

Je marche.	I walk./I am walking.
Tu marches?	Are you walking?/Do you walk?

 It is not possible to create a verb form in French by translating literally "I am . . . ing."

(ii)   The present tense in French is used:

(A) To express what the situation is now:

Nous passons quelques semaines en Provence.	We are spending a few weeks in Provence.

In cases where the emphasis is on a continuing action at this moment, use **en train de** + infinitive.

Je suis en train d'écrire des cartes postales à tous mes amis.	I'm in the process of writing cards to all my friends.

(B) To express what happens sometimes or usually:

Nous louons cette maison tous les ans.	We rent this house every year.

(C) To express what is going to happen in the future:

Nous rentrons à Paris la semaine prochaine.	We go back to Paris next week.

Note: In both French and English it is possible - and normal - to express future tense ideas using the present tense.

(D) To express what has been happening up until now and may be going to continue, using **depuis**, or **depuis que**, "since."

Il *fait* un temps superbe depuis que nous sommes arrivés, mais depuis hier le temps *devient* orageux.	The weather *has been* superb ever since we arrived, but since yesterday it *has become* thundery.

 This is an occasion where different tenses are used in French and English. Note also that in English the word *since* is often absent, or is replaced by *for*.

Nous sommes ici depuis un mois.	We have been here (for) a month.

 In negative sentences, however, **depuis** is followed by a past tense:

Nous *n'avons pas eu* de pluie *depuis* six mois.	We *have not had* any rain *for* six months.

Depuis is also used with the imperfect tense [➤12c(iv)].

Where there is a need to place emphasis on the time elapsed, the following expressions are useful, and would be preferred to **depuis**, which would not be used to open a sentence emphatically:

Voilà une heure qu'on attend.	We've been waiting for an hour.
Ça fait une heure qu'on attend.	
Il y a une heure qu'on attend.	

(E) In **je viens de** + infinitive. The present tense of **venir** is frequently used in the construction **venir de** (**faire quelque chose**) to convey an action in the recent past, the equivalent of the English "to have just."

Je viens de cueillir des prunes.	I've just picked some plums.

Venir de + infinitive is also used in a similar way in the imperfect tense [➤12c(iv)].

(F) To form the historic present. The present tense in French is often used with the value of a past tense, especially in newspaper reporting; this occurs to a lesser extent in English newspapers, where it tends to be limited to headlines of the type President Signs New Deal on Europe. Known as the historic present, this use of the present tense is illustrated below. Note the choice of the imperfect tense for **détenait**, which confirms that the historic present is considered a past tense in terms of the sequence of tenses:

Le Britannique Nigel Mansell (Williams-Renault) *remporte* **le grand prix du Portugal de Formule 1, devant l'Autrichien Gerhard Berger et le Brésilien Ayrton Senna, tous deux sur Marlborough McLaren Honda. Avec ce neuvième succès, Mansell** *bat* **le record de victoires en une saison qu'il** *détenait* **conjointement avec Senna.**	Briton Nigel Mansell (Williams-Renault) *has won* the Portuguese Grand Prix for Formula 1, ahead of the Austrian Gerhard Berger and the Brazilian Ayrton Senna, both driving Marlborough McLaren Honda cars. With this ninth win, Mansell *broke* the record for the number of victories in a season, which he *held* jointly with Senna.

12b The perfect tense

➤ [For details of the formation of the perfect tense ➤16b; for auxiliary verbs with the perfect tense ➤11c; and for past participle agreements ➤11d.]

The perfect tense in French has two uses. One matches closely the English perfect tense (e.g., I have spoken). The other replaces the simple past or past historic tense (e.g., I spoke) which in French is known as the *passé simple* [more on the past historic ➤12d] and is not generally used in speech.

(i) The perfect tense can be used to convey the idea of an event that has happened but still relates in some way to the here and now:

J'ai perdu un gant. Est-ce que tu l'as vu?	I've lost a glove. Have you seen it?

Even though this is a past tense, the actions are still very much of the present. The next part of the conversation may very well be:

Je l'ai trouvé!	I've found it!

Related to this first use of the perfect tense is the pluperfect tense, which in form differs from the perfect tense only in that the auxiliary is in the imperfect instead of the present:

J'avais perdu un gant. **J'étais montée voir si je l'avais laissé dans notre chambre.**	I had lost a glove. I had gone upstairs to see if I had left it in our bedroom.

(ii) In speech and informal writing the perfect tense in French doubles for the simple past tense [past historic ➤12d], which is limited to written narrative and other formal language:

Nous *avons quitté* le théâtre vers onze heures, nous *avons pris* un taxi, et nous *sommes arrivés* à la maison vers onze heures et demie.	We *left* the theater at about eleven, we *took* a taxi, and we *arrived* at the house at about half past eleven.

Note that the actions in the above example are single events. Where a past tense needs to convey the idea of repeated events in the past, the imperfect tense is used:

Tous les soirs, je *quittais* le théâtre vers onze heures et je *prenais* un taxi pour rentrer chez moi.	Evening evening I *left* the theater at about eleven and *took* a taxi home.

➤ [For details of this use of the imperfect tense ➤12c].

The sense of the perfect tense is also conveyed by **je viens de** + infinitive, "I have just." [➤12a(v)].

12c   The imperfect tense

The word *imperfect* as used here comes from the Latin *imperfectus* meaning "incomplete." This gives us a clue to one of the principal uses of this tense in French.

The imperfect is used:

(i)   To indicate something that was uncompleted or continuing, or that was interrupted by another event:

Moi, je *dormais* dans le fauteuil, et ma femme *travaillait* à l'ordinateur, quand les enfants sont rentrés. **Il *faisait* déjà nuit.**	I *was asleep* in the armchair, and my wife *was working* at the computer, when the children got back. It *was* already dark.

(ii)   To indicate something repeated or regular in the past:

Normalement je *passais* mes weekends à travailler au jardin.	Normally I *spent* my weekends working in the yard/garden. (Normally I *would spend* . . . or Normally I *used to spend* . . .)

 As the above examples show, the imperfect is expressed in English in a number of forms. When the English is in the form "was/were doing," the choice of the imperfect in French is straightforward. Care is needed, however, on the many occasions where the English form suggests another tense as in "spent/would spend," above.

VERBS

(iii)   In some conditional sentences with **si**:

Si je *connaissais* **son adresse, j'irais le voir.**	*If* I *knew* his address, I would go and see him.

➤   [For full details of conditional sentences ➤12g.]

(iv)   With **depuis**, **depuis que**, "since, for,"

J'habitais **le quartier** depuis **quelques années.**	I *had lived* in the area *for* some years.

 The above example means literally "I was living in the area since some years." This use of a different tense in English and French occurs also in the present tense, and applies also to the use of **il y a** and **venir de** (➤12a(iv–v)).

Il y avait dix jours que les enfants étaient en vacances. Je venais de les emmener voir leurs grand-parents.	The children had been on vacation for ten days. I had just taken them to see their grandparents.

(v)   In indirect speech or with indirect questions in the past tense:

Quand je lui ai demandé ce qu'il faisait **dans la vie, il m'a dit qu'il** travaillait **dans le tourisme.**	When I asked him what he *did* for a living, he said he *worked* in tourism.

12d   The past historic tense

The past historic tense is the original tense used to describe past events in French:

Le train s'arrêta. **Tout le monde** descendit. **Les douaniers** inspectèrent **les passeports des voyageurs.**	The train *stopped*. Everyone *got out*. The border officials *inspected* the travelers' passports.

However, its use is now largely limited to literary and formal printed registers. In newspapers, speech, and informal writing, the perfect tense has now substantially replaced the past historic.

12e *The future tense*

(i) Expressing futurity

Futurity can be expressed in French in several ways:

• By the use of the present tense, especially when present intentions are being conveyed:

Nous *partons* le vingt-trois juillet.	We *are leaving* on the twenty-third of July. (it is our intention)

• By the use of the present tense of **aller** (to go) + infinitive, a use that corresponds closely to English, and also conveys present intentions:

Nous *allons visiter* trois continents en un mois.	We *are going to visit* three continents in one month.

• By the use of the future tense, which is frequently inter-changeable with the forms above, except that it does not nec-essarily carry the notion of present intention:

La nuit du dimanche, treize octobre, il n'y *aura* pas de lune.	On the night of Sunday, October thirteen, there *will be* no moon.

(ii) Future tense in conditional sentences

The future tense is used in conditional sentences [➤12g]:

Si j'ai d'autres nouvelles, je t'*écrirai*.	If I have any other news, I'*ll write* to you.

(iii) Warnings

Aller is preferred when giving warnings:

Attention! Tu *vas* te faire mal!	Careful! You'*ll* hurt yourself!

(iv) Quand, dès que + future tense

The future tense is required after a range of time words such as **quand** (when) and **dès que** (as soon as), where in English a present tense would be used:

Quand vous le *verrez*, est-ce que vous *pourrez* lui dire que je n'ai toujours pas eu de réponse à mon invitation? Oui, je le lui dirai dès que je le *verrai*.	When you *see* him, *can* you tell him that I still haven't had a reply to my invitation? Yes, I'll tell him as soon as I *see* him.

12f The future perfect tense

The future perfect tense is a compound tense using the auxiliary in the future tense + the past participle, to give the meaning "I shall have done something."

J'aurai terminé ce chapitre avant minuit.	I shall have finished this chapter before midnight.
Elle sera rentrée bien avant la cérémonie.	She will have returned well before the ceremony.

It is most often used in sentences involving time words such as **quand** (when) and **dès que** (as soon as). Somewhat illogically, such sentences do not use a future or future perfect tense in English, but a perfect tense. Particular care is therefore needed when expressing this idea in French:

Dès que j'aurai réparé la vitre cassée, nous nous mettrons en route.	As soon as I have repaired the broken window pane, we will get going.

This use of the future perfect corresponds exactly to the uses of the future tense detailed in 12e(iv), above.

12g The conditional and conditional perfect tenses

Conditional sentences are mostly introduced by **si** (if), **s'** before **il(s)**. Conditional sentences exist in French at three levels, as in English:

Si j'ai le temps, j'irai à la plage cet après-midi.	If I have the time, I shall go to the beach this afternoon. (*it's quite likely*)

| Si j'avais le temps, j'irais à la plage cet après-midi. | If I had the time, I would go to the beach this afternoon. (*it's uncertain*) |
| Si j'avais eu le temps, je serais allé à la plage cet après-midi. | If I had had the time, I would have gone to the beach this afternoon. (*but I didn't, and it's too late!*) |

The three levels illustrated above are levels of likelihood. The tenses correspond to those used in English:

si + present + future	(*most likely, if direct condition met*)
si + imperfect + conditional	(*less likely*)
si + pluperfect + perfect conditional	(*purely hypothetical*)

The same three levels of the use of the conditional are also valuable when responding to invitations or propositions and expressing preferences, though with a slightly different value:

Oui, je veux bien.	Yes, thanks! (*American English*) Yes, please! (*British English*)
Oui, j'aimerais bien.	Yes, I would like that. (*normal polite acceptance*)
J'aurais bien aimé, mais...	I would very much have liked to, but . . . (*polite refusal*)

Similarly the conditional and conditional perfect are used for polite requests:

| Je *voudrais* parler à monsieur le directeur. | I *would like* to speak to the (company) director. |
| J'*aurais voulu* demander un conseil à un de vos collègues. | I *would rather like* to ask one of your colleagues for some advice. |

12h   *The past anterior*

This tense is not used in current speech. It can be found in literary and other printed texts. It has the same meaning as the pluperfect [➤12b(i)] and is used after conjunctions of time (**quand**, **dès que**, etc.) when the past historic is used in the main clause:

Quand le juge *eut fini* de prononcer son jugement, le prisonnier *fut emmené*.

When the judge *had finished* pronouncing judgment, the prisoner *was taken away*.

⓵⓷ Requests and commands: the imperative

13a Formation

(i) The *imperative* (or more precisely the *imperative mood*) is used for a variety of purposes including commands, requests, warnings, instructions, invitations, and advice. It has three forms:

Réfléchis!	Think carefully!
Réfléchissez!	Think carefully!
Réfléchissons!	Let's think carefully!

The imperatives thus consist simply of the usual **tu**, **vous**, or **nous** form of the verb in the present tense, but without the pronoun. Verbs whose **tu** form ends in **-es** (e.g., regular **-er** verbs) drop the final **-s** in the **tu** form of the imperative:

Pense à tes amis.　　　Think of your friends.

The verb **aller** behaves in the same way.

Va chercher un journal.　　Go and fetch a newspaper.

 The above rule (omitting the final -s) does not apply before **y** and **en**:

Penses-y!　　　Think about it!
Demandes-en!　　Ask for some.

(ii) *Negative imperatives*

Negative imperatives are formed in the normal way:

N'oubliez pas l'heure.　　Don't forget the time.

[For the use and position of object pronouns with the imperative, ►21b(vii), (viii).]

(iii) No single-word equivalent exists in English for the first person plural imperative in French – hence the somewhat cumbersome translation "let us."

Particularly useful are **Allons-y!** (Let's go!) and **Voyons!** which either means "Let's see," or can be used to challenge another remark, in which case it has the value of "Don't be silly!"

13b   Uses of the imperative and other forms
(i)   Tone

Imperative does not necessarily imply "imperious." Imperatives are often used in French in friendly or informal contexts:

Venez prendre un apéritif ce soir.	Come and have a drink this evening.
Passe nous dire bonjour si tu as le temps.	Drop in and say hello if you have time.

(ii)   Instructions

In written instructions, recipes, and notices, the infinitive may be used:

Délayer le contenu du sachet dans un demi-litre d'eau et porter à ébullition.	Mix the contents of the package into half a litre of water and bring to a boil.

Note also **défense de** and **interdit**:

Défense de stationner.	No parking.
Pelouse interdite.	Do not walk on the grass.

(iii)   Veuillez

In formal documents and fixed phrases in letter-writing, **veuillez** (the imperative of **vouloir**) may be used:

Veuillez trouver ci-joint...	Please find enclosed . . .

(iv)   Tiens, tenez

Tiens and **tenez** are particularly useful. They have two distinct uses:

To attract someone's attention when giving or passing something:

Tiens, prends ton assiette.	Here, take your plate.
Tenez, il y a une lettre pour vous.	Here you are, there's a letter for you.

To express surprise. Only the **tiens** form can be used for this purpose:

Tiens, je n'aurais jamais cru cela possible.	Heavens, I would never have thought it possible.
Tiens, tiens.	Well, I never!

14 Areas of uncertainty: the subjunctive mood

14a What does the subjunctive do?

In general terms the distinction between the *subjunctive mood* and the *indicative mood* [➤12], is about the *stance* adopted toward the action, event, or state that the verb describes. In the indicative, the verb is thought of simply as an action, event, or state of affairs that has happened, is happening, or will happen, according to the tense used. The use of a subjunctive generally indicates the adoption of a particular emotional attitude (wish, fear, pleasure, uncertainty, etc.) toward the event. Compare the following sentences:

Il *gagnera* certainement le prix.	He will certainly win the prize. (*indicative, states fact*)
Je préfèrerais qu'il ne le *gagne* pas.	I would prefer him not to win it. (*subjunctive, expresses wish*)

Although this distinction between the indicative and subjunctive moods may help to explain the existence of the subjunctive, it would be unsafe to apply it as a rule when choosing the appropriate verb formulation, because of the many exceptions and constraints relating to the use of the subjunctive in French.

It is important, however, to keep the following points firmly in mind:

(i) Since in English the subjunctive exists only in residual or occasional forms (If that *be* the case, would that you *knew*, urge that he *reconsider*), the wording alone in English will not generally indicate when a subjunctive would be needed in French.

(ii) Although there are four subjunctive tenses in French [➤16b], in everyday use the subjunctive rarely occurs in any other tense than the present, and to a lesser extent the perfect (which is formed using the present subjunctive of the auxiliary).

(iii) For most purposes it is easier to think of the subjunctive as occurring after specified verbs and fixed phrases and in subordinate clauses [➤4e] beginning with **que**, meaning "that."

 The subjunctive is not generally used unless there is a change of subject in the sentence. If the subject is the same, other constructions such as the infinitive are generally preferred:

Hélène *préférerait que vous arriviez* **avant huit heures.**	Hélène would prefer you to arrive before eight o'clock.
Hélène *préférerait arriver* **avant huit heures.**	Hélène would prefer to arrive before eight o'clock.

In the first case above, a subjunctive is required after a verb expressing wish, but not in the second case because there is no change of subject. It is not possible to translate "Hélène would prefer *you to arrive*" by using an infinitive in French.

14b *The tenses of the subjunctive*

[For the formation of the subjunctive ➤16b.]

(i) *Present tense*

Of the four subjunctive tenses, only the present subjunctive – and to a lesser extent the perfect subjunctive — appear in regular everyday use. The present subjunctive is used even in conjunction with past tenses, where one would expect some form of past subjunctive:

Nous avions insisté pour qu'il *vienne.*	We had insisted that he *should come.*

(ii) *Perfect tense*

The perfect subjunctive occasionally appears in everyday use:

Nous sommes étonnés que tu *aies choisi* **une telle solution.**	We are astonished that you *should have chosen* such a solution.

(iii) Imperfect and pluperfect subjunctive

The imperfect and pluperfect subjunctive forms are never used in current speech. They can be found in written and printed sources, but during this century their use has declined.

14c The subjunctive after certain verbs

The subjunctive is used with the following categories of verbs, of which the most common examples are listed:

(i)

Verb constructions expressing emotions such as pleasure, surprise, disbelief, liking, disliking, disappointment, regret, anger, fear, etc., when followed by **que**:

être content/ravi/heureux que..	be pleased/delighted/happy that . . .
s'étonner que...	be astonished/surprised that . . .
être surpris/étonné que...	be astonished/surprised that . . .
être incroyable/bizarre que	be unbelievable, strange that . . .
être déçu que ...	be disappointed that . . .
regretter que...	be sorry, regret that . . .
être dommage que ...	be a shame/pity that . . .
avoir peur que...	fear that, be afraid that . . .
craindre que...	fear that, be afraid that . . .

Je suis très *déçu qu'*ils *ne viennent pas.*
*J'ai peur qu'*il *soit* trop tard.

I'm very *disappointed that* they *are not coming.*
I fear it *is* too late.

 Contrary to what one would expect, the verb **espérer** (to hope) is not followed by a subjunctive.

 As with many of the verbs in these lists, if the subject is the same in both halves of the sentence, an infinitive construction is preferred to the subjunctive:

Je suis très déçu *d'être* le seul à participer.
J'ai peur *d'arriver* en retard.

I'm very disappointed that I'm the only one taking part.
I'm afraid of arriving late.

(ii) Verbs of wishing, wanting, preferring, ordering, permitting, forbidding, awaiting, expecting, etc., when followed by **que**:

vouloir que...	wish, want . . .
souhaiter que...	wish . . .
désirer que...	want . . .
préférer que...	prefer . . .
aimer mieux que...	prefer . . .
insister pour que...	insist . . .
ordonner que...	order . . .
permettre que...	permit, allow . . .
défendre que...	forbid . . .
attendre que...	await . . .
s'attendre à ce que...	expect . . .

Elle a insisté pour que l'erreur soit corrigée.	She insisted that the error be corrected.
On souhaiterait que les locataires partent avant Noël.	We would like the tenants to leave before Christmas.

 As with many of the verbs in these lists, if the subject is the same in both halves of the sentence, an infinitive construction is preferred to the subjunctive:

Elle a insisté pour partir seule.	She insisted on going alone.
Je souhaiterais l'accompagner.	I would like to go with her.

(iii) Verb constructions expressing necessity, urgency, and importance, when followed by **que**:

il faut que...	it is necessary that . . .
il est nécessaire que...	it is necessary that . . .
il est indispensable que...	it is indispensable that . . .
il est essentiel que...	it is essential that . . .
il est urgent que...	it is urgent that . . .
il est important que...	it is important that . . .

Il est essentiel que je voie le directeur.	It is essential that I see the director.

VERBS

As with many of the verbs in these lists, if the subject is the same in both halves of the sentence, an infinitive construction is preferred to the subjunctive:

Il est essentiel de s'équiper d'une boussole.	It is essential to equip oneself with a compass.

(iv)   Verb constructions expressing possibility, uncertainty, doubt:

il se peut que...	it is possible that . . .
il est possible que...	it is possible that . . .
il est impossible que...	it is impossible that . . .
il n'est pas certain que...	it is not certain that . . .
douter que...	doubt that . . .

Also in this category are verbs that express doubt or uncertainty *by being used in the negative:*

Je ne crois pas que...	I don't believe . . .
Je ne pense pas que...	I don't think . . .
Je ne suis pas convaincu que...	I'm not convinced that . . .

Douter also exists as a reflexive verb, **se douter de/que** with a different (almost opposite) meaning: "to suspect that," "to think so." It occurs most frequently in the expression:

Je m'en doutais.	I thought so.

Which you need to distinguish from:

J'en doutais.	I doubted it.

When used with **que** + subordinate clause, **se douter** is normally followed by the indicative rather than the subjunctive:

Je me doutais qu'il nous *préparait* **une surprise.**	I guessed he was preparing a surprise for us.

14d   The subjunctive after certain conjunctions

The subjunctive is used after certain conjunctions, the most common of which are listed here:

afin que	so that, in order that
pour que	so that, in order that
bien que	although
quoique	although
à moins que	unless
avant que	before
après que	after
à condition que	on condition that, provided that
pourvu que	on condition that, provided that
de crainte que	for fear that
de peur que	for fear that
de façon que	so as to, with the intention that/of
de sorte que	so as to, with the intention that/of
de manière que	so as to, with the intention that/of
jusqu'à ce que	until
sans que	without

Afin que les clients puissent s'asseoir, le supermarché a installé des bancs.	So that customers can sit down, the supermarket has installed benches.
Nous pouvons donc nous asseoir, pourvu qu'il y ait de la place.	So we can sit down, provided there is room.

 With some of the expressions in this list, if the subject is the same in both halves of the sentence, an infinitive construction is preferred to the subjunctive:

Afin d'aider leurs clients, ils ont ouvert d'autres caisses.	So as to help their customers, they have opened new checkouts.
Ils l'ont fait sans l'annoncer.	They did it without announcing it.

But:

Ils l'ont fait sans que je le sache.	They did it without my knowing about it.

14e Other uses of the subjunctive

(i) As an extension of the need for a subjunctive after expressions of wish, it appears also in sentences where a relative clause specifies what one is looking for:

| Je voudrais une voiture qui *soit* luxueuse, durable, économique, nerveuse, et pas chère. J'aimerais un parfum que je *puisse* mettre en hiver et en été. | I'd like a car that would be luxurious, durable, economical, reponsive, and inexpensive. I'd like a perfume I can wear in winter and in summer. |

However, the subjunctive is only used in this sort of sentence when the idea relates to a requirement so far unachieved, and therefore not in the following case:

| J'ai trouvé un parfum que je peux mettre en hiver et en été. | I have found a perfume that I can wear in winter and in summer. |

(ii) The subjunctive is used in a relative clause following a superlative. Note that words such as **premier**, **dernier**, **seul**, and **unique** are treated as superlatives for this purpose:

| C'est l'inondation la plus catastrophique qu'ils *aient* jamais *eue*. Déménager, c'est la seule solution qu'ils *puissent* envisager. | It is the most catastrophic flood they have ever had. Moving out is the only solution they can envisage. |

(iii) As an extension of the need for the subjunctive after expressions of wish [>14c(ii)], the word **que** can be used to introduce a third-person command:

| Alors, qu'ils le fassent eux-mêmes! | Let them do it themselves, then! |

15 Things done to you: the passive

15a *What does the passive express?*

(i) Receivers and doers of action

In the passive, the subject of the verb is the receiver of the action of the verb, rather than the doer. Notice the difference between:

Il *énerve* ses collègues.	He *irritates* his colleagues. (*active*)

and

Il *est énervé* par ses collègues.	He *is irritated* by his colleagues. (*passive*)

(ii) Par, de

As you will see from the above example, the doer of the action in the passive is introduced through the word **par** (by). Sometimes **de** is used instead of **par**, when there is less emphasis on an action being done to the recipient:

Ils étaient suivis d'une vingtaine d'enfants.	They were followed by a score of children.

(iii) Omission of doer

The doer of the action is often omitted altogether.

Elle a été agressée devant la gare.	She was attacked outside the station.

Note from the above example that the past participle in passive constructions always agrees with the subject, which in this case is feminine singular.

15b Passive constructions: limitations of use in French

Passive constructions can be used in French *only* where the verb in the active form would take a *direct* object. Contrast this with English, where the passive is also widely used when an *indirect* object becomes the subject:

The children gave a present to the teacher.

can become

The teacher was given a present by the children.

In French, this passive construction is not possible, unless the direct object (in this case "a present") becomes the subject, which generally would produce an unsatisfactory distortion of emphasis:

Un cadeau a été donné au professeur par les enfants.	A present was given to the teacher by the children.

For English-speaking people learning French, therefore, it is important to remember that expressions such as "I was sent, given, offered (something)" cannot be expressed using a passive in French [➤8d, 8e for a list of verbs taking an indirect object]. You may have seen references in French textbooks or grammars to ways of avoiding the passive in French, which seems to imply that the French have a dislike of passive constructions. The reality is simply that, viewed from an English standpoint, there are fewer opportunities to use passives in French.

15c Alternatives to passive constructions

Given that less use is made of passives in French than in English, it is important to note how agent-less ideas are expressed. The following patterns are widely used:

(i) On

The pronoun **on** is used [➤21b(iii), (iv)]:

On m'a envoyé les détails du projet.	I have been sent details of the project.

(ii) *Reflexive verbs*

Reflexive verb forms are frequently employed to convey a passive idea in a way that has no exact equivalent in English:

C'est un produit qui se vend partout dans la région.	It is a product that is sold everywhere in this area.
Ça se dit souvent...	It is often said . . .

➤ [For further details of use of reflexive verbs ➤8c.]

Types of French verb

16a   Predictability: conjugating a verb

The whole set of a verb's stems and endings is known as its *conjugation*. The various parts of this set are predictable at several levels:

(i)   Regular verbs

With most verbs you can predict any part of any tense from the spelling of the infinitive, plus of course a knowledge of the rules! These are known as *regular* verbs. In French, there are three conjugations of regular verbs, each with a distinct infinitive ending:

First conjugation	**marcher** (to walk)
Second conjugation	**finir** (to finish)
Third conjugation	**vendre** (to sell)

By far the majority of French verbs are of the **-er** type. In addition, all newly coined verbs are automatically **-er** verbs, for example, **filmer** (to film).

(ii)   Irregular verbs

Verbs in which some parts cannot be predicted in this way are classified as *irregular*. Some of the most common verbs in French are irregular. [For tables of irregular verbs ➤17e, 17f.] Some irregular verbs form groups, so if you know one you can predict the forms of any of the others. For example **partir**, **sortir**, **mentir**, **dormir**, **se repentir**, and **servir** all behave in the same way [➤17f].

(iii)

Verbs that are compounds of a given base verb generally conjugate like the base verb. So, for example, **surprendre** (to surprise), **comprendre** (to understand), and **apprendre** (to learn) all follow the model of **prendre** (to take).

16b   How are the major groups of verbs conjugated?

In the formation of tenses in French there are many features that are common to all conjugations, and to both regular and irregular verbs. These will be evident from the descriptions of the rules for the formation of each tense. Frequent reference will be made to the *stem* of the infinitive: this is obtained in most cases by removing the **-er**, **-ir**, or **-re** ending from the infinitive:

Infinitive	*Stem*
marcher	**march-**
finir	**fin-**
vendre	**vend-**

(i) *Present tense*

This is the tense in which there is the greatest variety of forms, both between the conjugations and in the incidence of irregular forms. Regular forms are produced by adding the following endings to the stem of the infinitive:

	je	*tu*	*il/elle/on*	*nous*	*vous*	*ils/elles*
march(er)	-e	-es	-e	-ons	-ez	-ent
fin(ir)	-is	-is	-it	-issons	-issez	-issent
vend(re)	-s	-s	—	-ons	-ez	-ent

It is worth noting that the **nous** forms of regular verbs (and indeed most irregular verbs) always end in **-ons**, the **vous** forms in **-ez**, and the **ils/elles** forms in **-ent**.

(ii) *Imperfect tense*

All regular verbs (and irregular verbs except **être**) form their imperfect tense by dropping the **-ons** ending and adding a standard set of endings to the **nous** form of the present tense.

Infinitive	*First person plural, present*	*Imperfect*
march(er)	**nous march**ons	**je march**als, etc.
fin(ir)	**nous fin**issons	**je fin**issals, etc.
vend(re)	**nous vend**ons	**je vend**als, etc.

The endings are always:

-ais	-ais	-ait	-ions	-iez	-aient

With only a handful of exceptions, the present participle is formed from the same stem as the imperfect tense [➤10b].

(iii) *Future tense*

Regular verbs form their future tense by adding a standard set of endings to the infinitive (the infinitive is reduced by removing the final **-e** in **-re** verbs):

Infinitive	Future tense
marcher	**marcher**ai
finir	**finir**ai
vendr(e)	**vendr**ai

The endings are always:

-ai	-as	-a	-ons	-ez	-ont

In the case of irregular verbs, any variation is in the stem, not in the endings.

(iv) Conditional tense

For *all* verbs, both regular and irregular, the conditional is formed from the same stem as the future tense [➤(iii) above], replacing the standard set of future tense endings by the standard set of imperfect tense endings [➤(ii) above]:

Infinitive	Conditional tense
marcher	**je marcher**ais, etc.
finir	**je finir**ais, etc.
vendr(e)	**je vendr**ais, etc.

The endings are always those of the imperfect tense:

-ais	-ais	-ait	-ions	-iez	-aient

(v) Past historic

As with the present tense, the stem of the infinitive is the starting point:

Infinitive	Past historic					
march(er)	**je march**ai	-as	-a	âmes	-âtes	-èrent
fin(ir)	**je fin**is	-is	-it	-îmes	-îtes	-irent
vend(re)	**je vend**is	-is	-it	-îmes	-îtes	-irent

Note that regular **-ir** and **-re** verbs use the same endings in the past historic. A third set of similar endings, **-us**, **-us**, **-ut**, **-ûmes**, **-ûtes**, **-urent**, occurs with some irregular verbs. **Venir** and **tenir** have irregular endings [➤17f].

(vi) Present subjunctive

Regular verbs of all three conjugations form their present subjunctive by dropping the **-ent** ending and adding a standard set of endings to a stem formed from the **ils/elles** form of the present tense.

Infinitive	Third person plural, present	Present subjunctive
marcher	ils march**ent**	que je march**e**, etc.
finir	ils finiss**ent**	que je finiss**e**, etc.
vendre	ils vend**ent**	que je vend**e**, etc.

The endings for all regular and almost all irregular verbs are:

-e	-es	-e	-ions	-iez	-ent

In the case of irregular verbs, any variation is always in the stem rather than in the endings (except **avoir** and **être**, ➤17f).

(vii) *Imperfect subjunctive*

The imperfect subjunctive is formed from the past historical tense [➤(v) above] as follows:

• **-er** verbs:

march**asse**	-asses	-ât	-assions	-assiez	-assent

• **-ir** and **-re** verbs:

vend**isse**	-isses	-ît	-issions	-issiez	-issent

Those few irregular verbs that form their past historic in **-us**, etc, follow the same pattern in the imperfect subjunctive:

• **être** (to be):

que je fusse	que nous fussions
que tu fusses	que vous fussiez
que il/elle fût	que ils fussent

(viii) *Formation of compound tenses*

To form any compound tense, one needs to know

• The past participle of the verb;
• Whether the auxiliary is **avoir** or **être** [for a list ➤11c].

The past participle of regular verbs is formed from the stem of the infinitive plus the following endings:

march**er**	march**é**
fin**ir**	fin**i**
vend**re**	vend**u**

There are many irregular past participles.

Once the past participles and the auxiliary verb are known, all compound tenses follow standard patterns:

VERBS

Compound tense	Tense of auxiliary	Example
perfect	present	**j'ai marché** **je suis allé**
pluperfect	imperfect	**j'avais marché** **j'étais allé**
future perfect	future	**j'aurai marché** **je serai allé**
conditional perfect	conditional	**j'aurais marché** **je serais allé**
past anterior	past historic	**j'eus marché** **je fus allé**
perfect subjunctive	present subjunctive	**que j'aie marché** **que je sois allé**
pluperfect subjunctive	imperfect subjunctive	**que j'eusse marché** **que je fusse allé**

 In compound tenses the past participle agrees in certain cases with its subject or its direct object [➤11d].

[For details of the use of tenses ➤11 and 12].

17 Verb tables

17a Conjugation of regular -er verbs

All **-er** verbs are regular except:

• **Aller** (to go), **envoyer** (to send) [➤17f];
• A small number of verbs where the irregularity takes the form of minor spelling adjustments necessitated by changes in stress in pronunciation [➤17b].

A model verb from this group is **marcher**:

marcher (*to walk*)

Present participle	***Past participle***
marchant	marché

Imperative	
marche!	marchez! marchons!

Present	***Perfect***
je marche	j'ai marché
tu marches	tu as marché
il/elle marche	il/elle a marché
nous marchons	nous avons marché
vous marchez	vous avez marché
ils/elles marchent	ils/elles ont marché

Imperfect	***Pluperfect***
je marchais	j'avais marché
tu marchais	tu avais marché
il/elle marchait	il/elle avait marché
nous marchions	nous avions marché
vous marchiez	vous aviez marché
ils/elles marchaient	ils/elles avaient marché

Future	***Future perfect***
je marcherai	j'aurai marché
tu marcheras	tu auras marché
il/elle marchera	il/elle aura marché
nous marcherons	nous aurons marché
vous marcherez	vous aurez marché
ils/elles marcheront	ils/elles auront marché

Conditional
je marcherais
tu marcherais
il/elle marcherait
nous marcherions
vous marcheriez
ils/elles marcheraient

Conditional perfect
j'aurais marché
tu aurais marché
il/elle aurait marché
nous aurions marché
vous auriez marché
ils/elles auraient marché

Past historic (simple past)
je marchai
tu marchas
il/elle marcha
nous marchâmes
vous marchâtes
ils/elles marchèrent

Past anterior
j'eus marché
tu eus marché
il/elle eut marché
nous eûmes marché
vous eûtes marché
ils/elles eurent marché

Present subjunctive
je marche
tu marches
il/elle marche
nous marchions
vous marchiez
ils/elles marchent

Perfect subjunctive
j'vaie marché
tu aies marché
il/elle ait marché
nous ayons marché
vous ayez marché
ils/elles aient marché

Imperfect subjunctive
je marchasse
tu marchasses
il/elle marchât
nous marchassions
vous marchassiez
ils/elles marchassent

Pluperfect subjunctive
j'eusse marché
tu eusses marché
il/elle eût marché
nous eussions marché
vous eussiez marché
ils/elles eussent marché

17b Verbs ending in -er with minor changes

(i) Acheter and projeter

A number of otherwise regular **-er** verbs make minor changes to spelling or use accents to reflect changes in stress. For example, the verb **acheter** (to buy) is pronounced **ach'ter** in its infinitive form and in other forms with a similar rhythm of pronunciation (**achetons**, **achetais**, **acheté**, etc.) However, in some forms of **acheter**, the second syllable is stressed, and in this case the stress is indicated by the inclusion of a grave accent: **achète**, **achèterai**. Stress of this sort is generally present when the following pattern occurs at the end of the verb's stem:

e + consonant + **e**

Where this happens, the stress is sometimes indicated by an accent (or by the change of an accent from acute to grave), and sometimes by doubling the final consonant, as in the case of **projeter** (to project). This verb is pronounced **proj'ter** in its infinitive form, but in cases where the stress is placed on the second syllable the effect is achieved by doubling the consonant, to give **projette**.

(ii) *Illustrative examples*

• **acheter,** "to buy" (other examples: **geler,** " to freeze"; **peler,** "to peel")

Present	**Past participle**
j'achète	acheté
tu achètes	
il/elle achète	**Future**
nous achetons	achèterai
vous achetez	
ils/elles achètent	**Past historic**
	achetai

• **jeter,** "to throw" (other examples: **appeler,** "to call"; **rejeter,** "to reject")

Present	**Past participle**
j'jette	jeté
tu jettes	
il/elle jette	**Future**
nous jetons	jetterai
vous jetez	
ils/elles jettent	**Past historic**
	jetai

• **céder,** "to yield" (other examples: **espérer,** "to hope"; **déléguer,** " to delegate"; **accélérer,** "to accelerate")

Present	**Past participle**
j'cède	cédé
tu cèdes	
il/elle cède	**Future**
nous cédons	céderai
vous cédez	
ils/elles cèdent	**Past historic**
	cédai

(iii) *Verbs with infinitives in* **-yer**, **-cer**, **-ger**

• **payer,** "to pay" (other examples: **ennuyer,** "to annoy"; **appuyer,** "to lean")

Present
je paie
tu paies
il/elle paie
nous payons
vous payez
ils/elles paient

Past participle
payé

Future
paierai

Past Historic
payai

- **commencer,** "to begin" (other examples: **rincer,** "to rinse")
[For the use of cedilla in French spelling ➤2a(iv)c].

Present
je commence
tu commences
il/elle commence
nous commençons
vous commencez
ils/elles commencent

Imperfect
je commençais
tu commençais
il/elle commençait
nous commencions
vous commenciez
ils/elles commençaient

Past participle
commencé

Present participle
commençant

Future
commencerai

Past Historic
commençai

- **manger**, "to eat" (other examples: "**déranger**," "to disturb"; **plonger**, "to dive")

Present
je mange
tu manges
il/elle mange
nous mangeons
vous mangez
ils/elles mangent

Imperfect
je mangeais
tu mangeais
il/elle mangeait
nous mangions
vous mangiez
ils/elles mangeaient

Past participle
mangé

Present participle
mangeant

Future
mangerai

Past historic
mangeai

17c   *Conjugation of regular* -ir *verbs*

[For irregular **-ir** verbs ➤17f].

A model verb from this group is **finir**:

finir (to finish, to end)

Present participle
finissant

Past participle
fini

Imperative
finis! finissons! finissez!

Present	**Perfect**
je finis	j'ai fini
tu finis	tu as fini
il/elle finit	il/elle a fini
nous finissons	nous avons fini
vous finissez	vous avez fini
ils/elles finissent	ils/elles ont fini

Imperfect	**Pluperfect**
je finissais	j'avais fini
tu finissais	tu avais fini
il/elle finissait	il/elle avait fini
nous finissions	nous avions fini
vous finissiez	vous aviez fini
ils/elles finissaient	ils/elles avaient fini

Future	**Future perfect**
je finirai	j'aurai fini
tu finiras	tu auras fini
il/elle finira	il/elle aura fini
nous finirons	nous aurons fini
vous finirez	vous aurez fini
ils/elles finiront	ils/elles auront fini

Conditional	**Conditional perfect**	
je finirais	j'aurais	fini
tu finirais	tu aurais	fini
il/elle finirait	il/elle aurait	fini
nous finirions	nous aurions	fini
vous finiriez	vous auriez	fini
ils/elles finiraient	ils/elles auraient	fini

Past Historic (simple past)
je finis
tu finis
il/elle finit
nous finîmes
vous finîtes
ils/elles finirent

Past anterior
j'eus fini
tu eus fini
il/elle eut fini
nous eûmes fini
vous eûtes fini
ils/elles eurent fini

Present subjunctive
je finisse
tu finisses
il/elle finisse
nous finissions
vous finissiez
ils/elles finissent

Perfect subjunctive
j'aie fini
tu aies fini
il/elle ait fini
nous ayons fini
vous ayez fini
ils/elles aient fini

Imperfect subjunctive
je finisse
tu finisses
il/elle finît
nous finissions
vous finissiez
ils/elles finissent

Pluperfect subjunctive
j'eusse fini
tu eusses fini
il/elle eût fini
nous eussions fini
vous eussiez fini
ils/elles eussent fini

17d Conjugation of regular -re verbs

[For the conjugation of irregular **-re** verbs ➤17f].

A model verb from this group is **vendre**:

vendre (to sell)

Present participle
vendant

Past participle
vendu

Imperative
vends! vendons! vendez!

Present
je vends
tu vends
il/elle vend
nous vendons
vous vendez
ils/elles vendent

Perfect
j'ai vendu
tu as vendu
il/elle a vendu
nous avons vendu
vous avez vendu
ils/elles ont vendu

Imperfect
je vendais
tu vendais
il/elle vendait
nous vendions
vous vendiez
ils/elles vendaient

Pluperfect
j'avais vendu
tu avais vendu
il/elle avait vendu
nous avions vendu
vous aviez vendu
ils/elles avaient vendu

Future
je vendrai
tu vendras
il/elle vendra
nous vendrons
vous vendrez
ils/elles vendront

Future perfect
j'aurai vendu
tu auras vendu
il/elle aura vendu
nous aurons vendu
vous aurez vendu
ils/elles auront vendu

Conditional
je vendrais
tu vendrais
il/elle vendrait
nous vendrions
vous vendriez
ils/elles vendraient

Conditional perfect
j'aurais vendu
tu aurais vendu
il/elle aurait vendu
nous aurions vendu
vous auriez vendu
ils/elles auraient vendu

Past historic (simple past)
je vendis
tu vendis
il/elle vendit
nous vendîmes
vous vendîtes
ils/elles vendirent

Past anterior
j'eus vendu
tu eus vendu
il/elle eut vendu
nous eûmes vendu
vous eûtes vendu
ils/elles eurent vendu

Present subjunctive
je vende
tu vendes
il/elle vende
nous vendions
vous vendiez
ils/elles vendent

Perfect subjunctive
j'aie vendu
tu aies vendu
il/elle ait vendu
nous ayons vendu
vous ayez vendu
ils/elles aient vendu

Imperfect subjunctive
je vendisse
tu vendisses
il/elle vendit
nous vendissions
vous vendissiez
ils/elles vendissent

Pluperfect subjunctive
j'eusse vendu
tu eusses vendu
il/elle eût vendu
nous eussions vendu
vous eussiez vendu
ils/elles eussent vendu

Present subjunctive
je vende
tu vendes
il/elle vende
nous vendions
vous vendiez
ils/elles vendent

Perfect subjunctive
j'aie vendu
tu aies vendu
il/elle ait vendu
nous ayons vendu
vous ayez vendu
ils/elles aient vendu

Imperfect subjunctive
je vendisse
tu vendisses
il/elle vendît
nous vendissions
vous vendissiez
ils/elles vendissent

Pluperfect subjunctive
j'eusse vendu
tu eusses vendu
il/elle eût vendu
nous eussions vendu
vous eussiez vendu
ils/elles eussent vendu

17e *The irregular verbs* avoir *and* être

avoir (to have)

Present participle
ayant

Past participle
eu

Imperative
aie ayons ayez

Present
j'ai
tu as
il/elle a
nous avons
vous avez
ils/elles ont

Perfect
j'ai eu
tu as eu
il/elle a eu
nous avons eu
vous avez eu
ils/elles ont eu

Imperfect
j'avais
tu avais
il/elle avait
nous avions
vous aviez
ils/elles avaient

Future
j'aurai
tu auras
il/elle aura
nous aurons
vous aurez
ils/elles auront

Conditional
j'aurais
tu aurais
il/elle aurait
nous aurions
vous auriez
ils/elles auraient

Past historic
j'eus
tu eus
il/elle eut
nous eûmes
vous eûtes
ils/elles eurent

Present subjunctive
j'aie
tu aies
il/elle ait
nous ayons
vous ayez
ils/elles aient

Pluperfect
j'avais eu
tu avais eu
il/elle avait eu
nous avions eu
vous aviez eu
ils/elles avaient eu

Future perfect
j'aurai eu
tu auras eu
il/elle aura eu
nous aurons eu
vous aurez eu
ils/elles auront eu

Conditional perfect
j'aurais eu
tu aurais eu
il/elle aurait eu
nous aurions eu
vous auriez eu
ils/elles auraient eu

Past anterior
j'eus eu
tu eus eu
il/elle eut eu
nous eûmes eu
vous eûtes eu
ils/elles eurent eu

Perfect subjunctive
j'aie eu
tu aies eu
il/elle ait eu
nous ayons eu
vous ayez eu
ils/elles aient eu

Imperfect subjunctive
j'eusse
tu eusses
il/elle eût
nous eussions
vous eussiez
ils/elles eussent

Pluperfect subjunctive
j'eusse eu
tu eusses eu
il/elle eût eu
nous eussions eu
vous eussiez eu
ils/elles eussent eu

être (to be)

Present participle
étant

Past participle
été

Imperative
sois soyons soyez

Present
j'suis
tu es
il/elle est
nous sommes
vous êtes
ils/elles sont

Perfect
j'ai été
tu as été
il/elle a été
nous avons été
vous avez été
ils/elles ont été

Imperfect
j'étais
tu étais
il/elle était
nous étions
vous étiez
ils/elles étaient

Pluperfect
j'avais été
tu avais été
il/elle avait été
nous avions été
vous aviez été
ils/elles avaient été

Future
j'serai
tu seras
il/elle sera
nous serons
vous serez
ils/elles seront

Future perfect
j'aurai été
tu auras été
il/elle aura été
nous aurons été
vous aurez été
ils/elles auront été

Conditional

j'serais
tu serais
il/elle serait
nous serions
vous seriez
ils/elles seraient

Conditional perfect

j'aurais été
tu aurais été
il/elle aurait été
nous aurions été
vous auriez été
ils/elles auraient été

Past historic

j'fus
tu fus
il/elle fut
nous fûmes
vous fûtes
ils/elles furent

Past anterior

j'eus été
tu eus été
il/elle eut été
nous eûmes été
vous eûtes été
ils/elles eurent été

Present subjunctive

j'sois
tu sois
il/elle soit
nous soyons
vous soyez
ils/elles soient

Perfect subjunctive

j'aie été
tu aies été
il/elle ait été
nous ayons été
vous ayez été
ils/elles vaient été

Imperfect subjunctive

j'fusse
tu fusses
il/elle fût
nous fussions
vous fussiez
ils/elles fussent

Pluperfect subjunctive

j'eusse été
tu eusses été
il/elle eût été
nous eussions été
vous eussiez été
ils/elles eussent été

17f   *Other irregular verbs*

The following parts are given for all verbs in this list:

- present tense in full;
- past participle;
- future tense (first person);
- past historic (first person).

From these forms all other tenses can generally be derived [➤16].

Verbs that form their compound tenses with **être** are marked with an asterisk★.

VERBS

Infinitive	Present	(a) Past participle (b) Future (c) Past historic
acquérir (to aquire)	acquiers acquiers acquiert acquérons acquérez acquièrent	(a) acquis (b) acquerrai (c) acquis
accueillir (to welcome)	➤ **cueillir**	
admettre (to admit)	➤ **mettre**	
★ **aller** (to go)	vais vas va allons allez vont	(a) allé ★ (b) irai (c) allai
Present subjunctive:	aille allions	
apercevoir (to see, perceive, glimpse)	aperçois aperçois aperçoit apercevons apercevez aperçoivent	(a) aperçu (b) apercevrai (c) aperçus
apparaître (to appear)	➤ **connaître**	
apprendre (to learn)	➤ **prendre**	
★ **s'asseoir** (to sit down)	assieds assieds assied asseyons asseyez asseyent	(a) assis ★ (b) assiérai (c) assis

Infinitive	Present	(a) *Past participle* (b) *Future* (c) *Past historic*
atteindre (to reach)	atteins atteins atteint atteignons atteignez atteignent	(a) atteint (b) atteindrai (c) atteignis
battre (to beat)	bats bats bat battons battez battent	(a) battu (b) battrai (c) battis
boire (to drink)	bois bois boit buvons buvez boivent	(a) bu (b) boirai (c) bus
commettre (to commit)	➤ **mettre**	
comprendre (to understand)	➤ **prendre**	
conduire (to drive, lead)	conduis conduis conduit conduisons conduisez conduisent	(a) conduit (b) conduirai (c) conduisis
connaître (to know)	connais connais connaît connaissons connaissez connaissent	(a) connu (b) connaîtrai (c) connus
construire (to construct)	➤ **conduire**	
convaincre (to convince)	➤ **vaincre**	

VERBS

Infinitive	Present	(a) Past participle (b) Future (c) Past historic
coudre (to sew)	couds couds coud cousons cousez cousent	(a) cousu (b) coudrai (c) cousis
courir (to run)	cours cours court courons courez courent	(a) couru (b) courrai (c) courus
couvrir (to cover)	couvre couvres couvre couvrons couvrez couvrent	(a) couvert (b) couvrirai (c) couvris
craindre (to fear)	➤ **atteindre**	
croire (to believe)	crois crois croit croyons croyez croient	(a) cru (b) croirai (c) crus
croître (to grow)	croîs croîs croît croissons croissez croissent	(a) crû/crue (*feminine form*) (b) croîtrai (c) (*no past historic*)

Infinitive	Present	(a) *Past participle* (b) *Future* (c) *Past historic*
cueillir (to pick, gather)	cueille cueilles cueille cueillons cueillez cueillent	(a) cueilli (b) cueillerai (c) cueillis
cuire (to cook)	➤ conduire	
décevoir (to disappoint)	➤ apercevoir	
découvrir (to discover)	➤ couvrir	
décrire (to describe)	➤ écrire	
détruire (to destroy)	➤ conduire	
devoir (to owe, have to)	dois dois doit devons devez doivent	(a) dû/due (*feminine form*) (b) devrai (c) dus
dire (to say)	dis dis dit disons dites disent	(a) dit (b) dirai (c) dis
dormir (to sleep)	dors dors dort dormons dormez dorment	(a) dormi (b) dormirai (c) dormis

VERBS

Infinitive	Present	(a) Past participle (b) Future (c) Past historic
écrire (to write)	écris écris écrit écrivons écrivez écrivent	(a) écrit (b) écrirai (c) écrivis
envoyer (to send)	envoie envoies envoie envoyons envoyez envoient	(a) envoyé (b) enverrai (c) envoyai
éteindre (to switch off)	➤ **atteindre**	
faire (to do, make)	fais fais fait faisons faites font	(a) fait (b) ferai (c) fis
Present subjunctive:	fasse fassions	
falloir (to must, be necessary)	il faut	(a) fallu (b) il faudra (c) il fallut
Present subjunctive:	qu il faille	
fuir (to flee)	fuis fuis fuit fuyons fuyez fuient	(a) fui (b) fuirai (c) fuis

Infinitive	Present	(a) *Past participle* (b) *Future* (c) *Past historic*
haïr (to hate)	hais hais hait haïssons haïssez haïssent	(a) haï (b) haïrai (c) haïs
introduire (to introduce)	➤ **conduire**	
joindre (to join)	➤ **atteindre**	
lire (to read)	lis lis lit lisons lisez lisent	(a) lu (b) lirai (c) lus
mentir (to tell lies, lie)	➤ **dormir**	
mettre (to put)	mets mets met mettons mettez mettent	(a) mis (b) mettrai (c) mis
moudre (to grind)	mouds mouds moud moulons moulez moulent	(a) moulu (b) moudrai (c) moulus
★ **mourir** (to die)	meurs meurs meurt mourons mourez meurent	(a) mort ★ (b) mourrai (c) mourus

VERBS

Infinitive	Present	(a) Past participle
		(b) Future
		(c) Past historic

★ naître (to be born)	nais	(a) né ★
	nais	
	naît	(b) naîtrai
	naissons	
	naissez	(c) naquis
	naissent	

nuire (to harm)	➤ conduire (past participle nui)	

offrir (to offer)	➤ couvrir	

ouvrir (to open)	➤ couvrir	

paraître (to appear)	➤ connaître	

★ partir (to leave)	➤ dormir	

peindre (to paint)	➤ atteindre	

plaindre (to pity)	➤ atteindre	

plaire (to please)	plais	(a) plu
	plais	
	plaît	(b) plairai
	plaisons	
	plaisez	(c) plus
	plaisent	

pleuvoir (to rain)	il pleut	(a) plu
		(b) il pleuvra
		(c) il plut

Present subjunctive:	qu il pleuve	

poursuivre (to pursue)	➤ suivre	

pouvoir (to be able)	peux (puis-je?)	(a) pu
	peux	
	peut	(b) pourrai
	pouvons	
	pouvez	(c) pus
	peuvent	

(**Puis-je?** *is used when the verb is inverted to form an interrogative.*)

Infinitive	Present	(a) *Past participle* (b) *Future* (c) *Past historic*
prendre (to take)	prends prends prend prenons prenez prennent	(a) pris (b) prendrai (c) pris
produire (to produce)	➤ **conduire**	
recevoir (to receive)	➤ **apercevoir**	
reconnaître (to recognize)	➤ **connaître**	
réduire (to reduce)	➤ **conduire**	
résoudre (to resolve)	résous résous résout résolvons résolvez résolvent	(a) résolu (b) résoudrai (c) résolus
rire (to laugh)	ris ris rit rions riez rient	(a) ri (b) rirai (c) ris
rompre (to break)	romps romps rompt rompons rompez rompent	(a) rompu (b) romprai (c) rompis

VERBS

Infinitive	Present	(a) *Past participle* (b) *Future* (c) *Past historic*
savoir (to know)	sais sais sait savons savez savent	(a) su (b) saurai (c) sus
Present subjunctive:	sache sachions	
Present participle:	sachant	
Imperative:	sache sachons sachez	
sentir (to feel)	➤ **dormir**	
servir (to serve)	➤ **dormir**	
★ **sortir** (to go out)	➤ **dormir**	
souffrir (to suffer)	➤ **couvrir**	
sourire (to smile)	➤ **rire**	
suivre (to follow)	suis suis suit suivons suivez suivent	(a) suivi (b) suivrai (c) suivis
surprendre (to surprise)	➤ **prendre**	
survivre (to survive)	➤ **vivre**	
★ **se taire** (to be quiet)	➤ **plaire** (*but* **il se tait** *has no circumflex on the* **i**)	
tenir (to hold)	➤ **venir**	
traduire (to translate)	➤ **conduire**	

Infinitive	Present	(a) Past participle (b) Future (c) Past historic
vaincre (to conquer)	vaincs vaincs vainc vainquons vainquez vainquent	(a) vaincu (b) vaincrai (c) vainquis
valoir (to be worth)	vaux vaux vaut valons valez valent	(a) valu (b) vaudrai (c) valus
Present subjunctive:	vaille valions	
★ **venir** (to come)	viens viens vient venons venez viennent	(a) venu ★ (b) viendrai (c) vins vins vint vînmes vîntes vinrent

vêtir (to dress) (Generally only found in past participle **vêtu**.)

vivre (to live)	vis vis vit vivons vivez vivent	(a) vécu (b) vivrai (c) vécus

VERBS

Infinitive	Present	(a) **Past participle** (b) **Future** (c) **Past historic**
voir (to see)	vois vois voit voyons voyez voient	(a) vu (b) verrai (c) vis
vouloir (to wish)	veux veux veut voulons voulez veulent	(a) voulu (b) voudrai (c) voulus
Present subjunctive:	veuille voulions	
Imperative:	veuille veuillez	

D

PEOPLE, THINGS, AND IDEAS: NOUNS AND NOUN PHRASES

Labeling the world: nouns

18a What does a noun do?

Nouns are the labels we attach to everything in the world around us or in our own minds: people, animals, things, events, processes, ideas. The nouns are highlighted in the following passage:

Ma *fille* ainée est *professeur* de sciences naturelles à l'*Université* de Lille.	My eldest *daughter* is a *teacher* of natural *science* at the *University* of Lille.

18b Adding detail: the noun phrase

More often than not, nouns have other words or groups of words (phrases or clauses) attached to them, to constitute what is known as a noun phrase. The additional items may take the form of:

- determiners [➤19];
- adjectives and adjectival phrases [➤20];
- relative clauses [➤21];
- prepositional phrases [➤23].

To avoid repetition, nouns (and therefore noun phrases) are often replaced by pronouns [➤21].

18c Proper and common nouns

(i) Proper nouns

A *proper noun* is the name of a particular person, place, or thing. For example:

Jeanne d'Arc, Jacques Delors, Vincent van Gogh
L'Arc de Triomphe, les Alpes, l'Australie
Le Martini, le Tour de France, l'Opéra de Paris

All other nouns are known as *common nouns*.

(ii) Use of capital letters

There are some cases in French where capital letters are not used with proper nouns [days of the week, months of the year, names of languages, and nouns of nationality ➤2a(ii)].

(iii)

It is worth remembering also that while some names are always proper nouns, such as **Paris, Jacques, Martini**, others may be used as common nouns on other occasions, e.g.

La maison blanche au coin de la rue est à vendre.	The white house on the corner is for sale.

but

La Maison Blanche est la résidence du président des Etats-Unis.	The White House is the residence of the president of the United States.

18d Gender of nouns in French

In English grammar, the term *gender* has a direct association with the sex of the noun. Masculine nouns refer to males (e.g., father, nephew, prince, actor, bull, rooster) and feminine nouns to females (mother, niece, princess, actress, cow, hen). Of course, the vast majority of nouns in English do not designate gender and are therefore neither masculine nor feminine.

However, in French grammar *all* nouns are classified as either masculine or feminine. As one would expect, most nouns denoting males are masculine in French, and most denoting females are feminine. But all other nouns are also classified as of masculine or feminine gender according to a variety of factors unconnected with notions of male and female, such as the word's origin, its spelling, or its meaning.

As in all languages, there are many illogicalities and exceptions, but there are some broad rules that can be useful aids to remembering the gender of nouns. Above all, it is worth getting into the habit of always learning a noun *complete with its article*, as an aid to memorization – for example, **une adresse**, not just **adresse**.

(i) Gender by meaning

• Days, months, and seasons are mostly MASCULINE:

NOUNS AND NOUN PHRASES

samedi	Saturday	**printemps**	spring
janvier	January		

• Metric weights, measures, and fractions are mostly MASCULINE:

un gramme	gram	**un quart**	quarter
un kilo	kilogram	**un dixième**	tenth
un mètre	meter		

• Trees and shrubs are mostly MASCULINE:

un chêne	oak	**un troène**	privet
un hêtre	beech		

Exceptions: **une aubépine** (hawthorn); **une ronce** (bramble).

• Countries and rivers ending in **-e** (as most do) are mostly FEMININE:

la Grande-Bretagne	Great Britain
la Loire	the Loire

Exceptions: **le Mexique** (Mexico); **le Rhône** (the Rhône).

• Countries and rivers not ending in **-e** are mostly MASCULINE:

le Canada	Canada	**le Niger**	Niger

• Vegetables and fruit ending in **-e** (as most do) are mostly FEMININE:

une tomate	tomato
une pomme	apple
une aubergine	eggplant

• Vegetables and fruit not ending in **-e** are mostly MASCULINE:

un chou	cabbage	**un citron**	lemon

• Trades, professions, subjects of study, areas of knowledge, and the arts are mostly FEMININE:

la plomberie	plumbing	**l'astronomie**	astronomy
l'architecture	architecture	**la peinture**	painting
la biologie	biology		

• Metals are mostly MASCULINE:

l'or	gold	**le cuivre**	copper
le plomb	lead		

• Languages are always MASCULINE:

le latin	Latin	**l'allemand**	German
le russe	Russian		

• Words recently introduced from English are mostly MASCULINE:

le sweatshirt   **le leader**   **le chewing gum**   **le rock**

(ii)   Gender by spellings and endings

• Nouns with the following endings are generally MASCULINE:

-age
le chômage	unemployment
le chauffage central	central heating

Exceptions: **une image** plus a few mainly single-syllable words such as **une cage** (cage), **la rage** (rage; rabies), **la plage** (beach), **une page** (book page).

-ail
le travail	work
un vitrail	stained glass window

-sme
le communisme	communism
l'athlétisme	athletics
un microcosme	microcosm

-eau
un plateau	tray
un couteau	knife
un bateau	boat

Exceptions: **l'eau** (**water**), **la peau** (skin).

-ège
un collège	school or college
un cortège	procession

-ème
un système	system
un problème	problem

-ment
le gouvernement	government
un vêtement	garment

• Nouns with the following endings are usually FEMININE:

-aison
une combinaison	slip; overalls
une maison	house

-ance, -anse, -ence, -ense (*all pronounced identically*)
l'importance	importance
une danse	dance
une absence	absence
une dépense	item of expenditure

-ation
une nation	nation
une illustration	illustration

-ion
une mission	mission
la passion	passion

-te, -tte
une date	date (time)
une datte	date (fruit)
une tablette	small table

-ure
la nourriture	food
la fourrure	fur

(iii)   Gender of animals

For all but some of the most common animals, a single noun form exists, of which the gender cannot be changed:

***un* éléphant**	elephant	***une* girafe**	giraffe

To express the idea of a female elephant, one has to say **un éléphant femelle.** To express the idea of a male giraffe, one has to say **une girafe mâle.**

This requirement holds good for the names of most animals. However, the names of some animals have both masculine and feminine variants, for example:

un chat	**une chatte**	cat
un chien	**une chienne**	dog
un âne	**une ânesse**	donkey
un canard	**une canne**	duck

In many cases, as in English, quite different words are used for the male and female animal:

un bouc	billygoat	**une chèvre**	she-goat

Where two different forms exist, one (generally the masculine) is used as the general term. Note, however, that in the above example, the general term for a goat is the feminine **une chèvre.**

In a few cases, in addition to a masculine and a feminine form, a separate word exists for the general description:

un bélier	ram	**un coq**	cockerel
une brebis	ewe	**une poule**	hen
un mouton	sheep	**un poulet**	chicken

(iv) *Masculine-feminine variants*

In many cases, nouns have masculine and feminine variants, formed generally by the same rules as apply to adjectives:

un ouvrier	**une ouvrière**	worker
un cousin	**une cousine**	cousin
un ami	**une amie**	friend
un pharmacien	**une pharmacienne**	pharmacist, druggist

[For a full description of masculine-feminine endings ➤20].

(v) *Professions*

Some nouns exist only in one gender, regardless of the sex of the person described. The most frequently encountered examples are:

un médecin	doctor
un auteur	author
un écrivain	writer
un ingénieur	engineer
un professeur	teacher (secondary school and beyond)
un ministre	minister
un juge	judge
un magistrat	examining magistrate
un facteur	postal worker, letter carrier

With changing social attitudes to women, nominally incorrect forms such as **une professeur, une ministre** are increasingly encountered. However, in most cases where a feminine version is required, the above professions and jobs are varied: **une femme ingénieur.**

(vi)   Invariable forms

Other invariable forms exist, unrelated to professions for example:

• Always MASCULINE:

un guide	guide	un témoin	witness
un ange	angel	un assassin	killer

• Always FEMININE:

une personne	person
une victime	victim
une vedette	star (personality)

18e   One or more? Plural of nouns

(i)   Adding -s

In French, as in English, the standard way of making a noun plural is by adding an **-s**:

un timbre	des timbres	stamps
une lettre	des lettres	letters
une adresse	des adresses	addresses

However, the final **-s** is silent in most cases in spoken French, so plurals are distinguished not by the sound of the noun, which in most cases remains unchanged, but by the words immediately associated with it:

Je vais signer _la_ lettre avant de partir.	I'll sign the letter before I go.
Je vais signer _les_ lettres avant de partir.	I'll sign the letters before I go.

In the English sentences above, the audible difference is between _letter_ and _letters_; in the French sentences, the audible difference is between **la** and **les**.

(ii)   Other plurals

The following types of noun do not add **-s** for their plural:

• Singular in **-al**; plural in **-aux**:

un journal	des journaux	newspaper(s)
un canal	des canaux	canal(s)
un cheval	des chevaux	horse(s)

Common exceptions are:

un festival	**des festivals**	festival(s)
un bal	**des bals**	dance(s)
un carnaval	**des carnavals**	carnival(s)

• Singular in **-au, -eau, -eu**: add **-x** to form the plural:

un tuyau	**des tuyaux**	pipe(s)
un manteau	**des manteaux**	coat(s)
un neveu	**des neveux**	nephew(s)

Exception: **un pneu, des pneus** (tire[s]).

• The following nouns ending in **-ou** form their plural with **-x** instead of **-s**:

un bijou	**des bijoux**	jewel(s)
un caillou	**des cailloux**	pebble(s)
un chou	**des choux**	cabbage(s)
un genou	**des genoux**	knee(s)
un hibou	**des hiboux**	owl(s)
un joujou	**des joujoux**	toy(s)
un pou	**des poux**	louse, lice

• Where the singular noun ends in **-s, -z**, or **-x,** there is no change in the plural:

un matelas	**des matelas**	mattress(es)
un nez	**des nez**	nose(s)
un prix	**des prix**	price(s)

• Family names are unchanged in the plural:

Les Dupont ont déménagé hier.	The Duponts moved out yesterday.

(iii)   Plural of compound nouns

Compound nouns in French are generally formed by combining two words, using a hyphen:

un porte-monnaie   purse   **un gratte-ciel**   skyscraper

There are many inconsistencies in deriving plural forms of compound nouns, which are best learned individually. As a general principle, however, verb + noun compounds do not change in the plural:

un/des porte-monnaie		purse(s)
un/des gratte-ciel		sky-scraper(s)
un/des passe-partout		masterkey(s)

but

un tire-bouchon	des tire-bouchons	corkscrew(s)
un essuie-glace	des essuie-glaces	windshield wipers
un/des pare-chocs		car bumper(s)

Where compounds are made up of noun + noun or adjective + noun, both parts become plural:

une porte-fenêtre	des portes-fenêtres	french window(s)
un chou-fleur	des choux-fleurs	cauliflowers

Where compounds are made up of preposition + noun, the plural is the same as the singular:

un hors d'oeuvre	des hors d'oeuvre	appetizer(s)

18f Adjectives used as nouns

Adjectives are regularly used in French as nouns.

(i) Implied noun

Sometimes the noun is strongly implied:

Pour la photo, mettons les petits devant et les grands derrière.	For the photo let's have the little ones at the front and the grown-ups at the back.
Le plus urgent, c'est de contacter les parents.	The most urgent thing is to contact the parents.

Male-female distinction is often expressed using adjectives as nouns:

une vieille	an old woman
un jeune aveugle	a young blind man

(ii) Abstract nouns

Adjectives can also stand alone to represent abstract nouns. In this case they are masculine:

| Il ne sait pas distinguer le vrai du le faux. | He cannot tell the difference between truth and falsehood. |

18g Nouns formed from other parts of speech

Prepositions are occasionally used as nouns in French:

le pour et le contre   the arguments for and against

[For verbs used as nouns ➤10a(iii)].

19 Specifying nouns: determiners

19a What are determiners?

You will not find the word *determiner* in older grammars, but it is a very useful term, that includes some of the most common words in any language. Determiners are used with nouns to place them in a context, to say whether they are assumed to be known or not, to whom they belong, how many there are, and so on. So, for example, a noun such as **voiture** (car) can be introduced by different determiners according to the context:

La voiture était sale.	*The* car was dirty. (*not just any car, but a particular one*)
Il me faut *une* voiture.	I need *a* car. (*not specified – could be any car*)
Cette voiture a un toit ouvrant.	*This* car has a sunroof. (*emphatic reference to a particular car*)
Notre voiture est trop petite.	*Our* car is too small. (*belongs to us*)
Nos voisins ont *trois* voitures.	Our neighbors have *three* cars. (*number specified*)
Quels voisins?	*Which* neighbors? (*asking for specification*)

However, these examples remind us that there is an important difference between French and English in the use of determiners. The form of most determiners in French has to *agree with* the noun; that is, it may vary according to whether the noun is masculine or feminine (gender), singular or plural (number).

19b The interrogative determiner quel, *"which"* or *"what"*

	Singular	*Plural*
Masculine	**quel**	**quels**
Feminine	**quelle**	**quelles**

Quel chemin prenons-nous?	Which way are we going?
Quelle heure est-il?	What time is it?
Quels endroits veux-tu voir?	What places do you want to see?
Quelles idées as-tu?	What ideas do you have?

Quel can be used in both direct and indirect questions [➤5d].

Quelle route préfères-tu?	Which road do you prefer?
Il n'a pas dit quelle route il prenait.	He didn't say which road he was taking.

Quel can be separated from its noun by a form of the verb **être:**

Quels sont tes projets pour aujourd'hui?	What are your plans for today?

19c   *Already known: the definite article* le, la, les

The definite article is used most frequently in English to introduce nouns that refer to specific items, either because they have already been mentioned or because it is obvious from the context that one is referring to a particular item. In French, the definite article has an additional important use that has no equivalent in English, in that it is placed before the many nouns where in English no article would be required. This is described elsewhere in this chapter [➤19b].

(i)   *Forms*

The definite article has the following forms:

	Singular	Plural
Before masculine nouns	**le, l'**	**les**
Before feminine nouns	**la, l'**	**les**

(ii)   *Abbreviated form, l'*

The shortened form **l'** is used instead of **le** or **la** before a word beginning with a vowel or mute **h** [➤2a(i)], to reflect the pronunciation:

l'enfant	the child	**l'homme**	the man

NOUNS AND NOUN PHRASES

Note that **l'** is not used with plural forms. Instead, the **-s** on **les** is elided and pronounced as **z**:

les enfants   the children   **les hommes**   the men

(iii)   *à, de + definitive article*

When the prepositions **à** and **de** are used in front of the definite article forms **le** and **les**, they combine to produce the compound forms below.

à + le →	**au**	de + le →	**du**
à + les →	**aux**	de + les →	**des**

The **la** and **l'** forms are unaffected.

Je vais *au* bureau ce matin.	I'm going *to the* office this morning.
Je passerai *à la* boulangerie.	I'll call in *at the* bakery.
Je dirai bonjour *aux* voisins.	I'll say hello *to the* neighbors.
J'arriverai *à l'*heure.	I'll arrive *on* time.
Je rentre souvent tard *du* bureau.	I'm often late back *from the* office.
Je regarde la tête *des* voyageurs.	I look at the faces *of the* passengers.
C'est la fin *de la* journée.	It's the end *of the* day.

(iv)   *Use of the definitive article*

The definite article is used in French:

(A) As in English, to make it clear that a particular item is being referred to:

N'oubliez pas *la* clé.	Don't forget the key.
Avez-vous fermé *les* fenêtres?	Have you closed the windows?

(B) When generalizing or using abstract nouns:

***Le* vin coûte moins cher en France.**	Wine is cheaper in France.
Je n'aime pas tellement *la* bière.	I don't like beer much.
***La* politique ne m'intéresse pas.**	Politics don't interest me.
Tant qu'il y a de *la* vie, il y a de *l'*espoir.	Where there's life, there's hope.

You will see from the above examples that in English the article is often omitted altogether when generalizing or using abstract terms. Remember, this is not possible in French.

(C) When expressing speeds and prices per quantity (in English the indefinite article "a" or "an" is used here):

Nous roulons à 120 kilomètres *à* l'heure.	We're doing 120 kilometers *an* hour.
Ce fromage est à 70 francs *le* kilo.	This cheese is 70 francs *a* kilo.
Le tissu bleu marine est à 80 francs *le* mètre.	The navy blue fabric costs 80 francs *a* meter.

(D) When referring to parts of the body, particularly when they are the object of a verb, or with reflexive verbs:

Ferme *les* yeux!	Close *your* eyes!
Tu peux me gratter *le* dos?	Can you scratch *my* back?
J'ai *la* tête qui tourne.	*My* head is spinning.
Donne-moi *la* main.	Give me *your* hand.
Je me suis lavé *la* figure.	I washed *my* face.
Il se ronge *les* ongles.	He bites *his* nails.

(E) When referring to names of countries and other named geographical features:

J'adore *la* France, et surtout *la* Provence.	I love France, especially Provence.
Vous connaissez *le* Mont Ventoux?	Do you know Mount Ventoux?

(F) When referring to languages:

Est-ce que *l'*espagnol est plus facile que *le* français?	Is Spanish easier than French?

Note, however, that with the verb **parler** the article is not present, unless the verb is qualified, for example, by an adverb:

Elle parle espagnol, couramment, mais elle parle très mal *le* russe.	She speaks Spanish fluently, but she speaks Russian very badly.

19d   The demonstrative determiner: ce, cet(te), ces

	Singular	Plural
Masculine	ce, cet	ces
Feminine	cette	ces

The form **cet** in the masculine singular is used before a vowel or mute **h**.

Demonstratives are like a strong definite article. While they are a means of being very specific about place and immediacy in English, their use in French is less complex:

Ce bouquin que tu as acheté hier, tu peux me le montrer?	That book you bought yesterday, can you show it to me?
Ce bouquin que tu as acheté hier, je le trouve très intéressant.	This book you bought yesterday, I find it very interesting.

It is clear from the above examples that whereas English distinguishes between "this" and "that," the French **ce** does not. To do so in French requires the additional use of the emphatic suffixes -**ci** and -**là**:

Moi je préfère cette table-*là*: cette table-*ci* est trop près de la porte.	I prefer *that* table: *this* table is too near the door.

19e   Unknown individuals: the indefinite article un, une, des

(i)   Forms

The indefinite article has three forms:

	Singular	Plural
Masculine	un	des
Feminine	une	des

(ii)   Use

When the indefinite article is used we know what type of person or thing the noun refers to but not which individual.

Il y a longtemps que je n'ai pas vu *un* bon film. Est-ce qu'il y a *un* cinéma en ville?	It's a long time since I saw a good movie. Is there a movie theater in town?

| Il y a *des* boîtes de nuit, mais je ne sais pas s'il y a *un* cinéma. | There are nightclubs, but I don't know whether there is a movie theater. |

(iii) *Etre* + *profession*

The indefinite article is not used after the verb **être** + the name of a job or profession:

| Il est médecin. | He is a doctor. |

However, after **c'est**, the article is required:

| C'est un médecin. | He is a doctor. |

The above sentences are identical in meaning. However, if the noun is qualified by an adjective, **C'est** must be used:

| C'est un très bon médecin. | He is a very good doctor. |

19f *Unknown quantities: the partitive article*

(i) *Du, de la, de l'*

The partitive article has three forms **du**, **de la**, and **de l'**. It is broadly equivalent to the English "some" or "any," though frequently no article is used in English where one would be required in French:

Il y a *du* miel et *de la* confiture sur la table.	There's honey and jam on the table.
J'ai mis aussi *du* yaourt.	I've put out some yogurt as well.
Avons-nous *de la* confiture d'orange?	Do we have any marmalade?
Si tu me donnes *de* l'argent, j'en achèterai ce matin.	If you give me some money, I'll buy some this morning.

(ii) *Quantity* + *de*

The partitive and indefinite article forms **du, de la, des** are reduced to **de** after expressions of quantity, such as:

131

beaucoup *de* **viande**	a lot of meat
très peu *de* **légumes**	very few vegetables
trop *de* **matière grasse**	too much fat content
assez *de* **sel**	enough salt
un verre *d'*eau	a glass of water
une bouteille *de* **vin**	a bottle of wine

Exceptions: **encore** (more); **bien** (many); **la plupart** (the majority, most).

–**Encore** *du* **vin, chers amis!**	"More wine, friends!"
Dans bien *des* **cas c'est différent.**	In many cases it's different.
La plupart *de* **mes amis ne fument plus.**	Most of my friends no longer smoke.
La plupart *du* **temps a été consacrée à la lecture.**	Most of the time was spent reading.

As the above examples illustrate, **la plupart** is treated as a plural when followed by a plural noun.

(iii)   *Negative quantities*

Pas de is best considered a negative expression of quantity. Accordingly, after a negative the indefinite article **un, une, des** and the partitive article **du, de la, de l'** are also replaced by **de** or **d'**:

Il n'y a pas *de* **sucre dans le bol.**	There isn't any sugar in the bowl.

The same applies to other negative forms used to express (negative) quantity:

Il ne reste plus *de* **vin.**	There's no wine left.
Il n'y a jamais *d'*eau fraîche dans le frigo.	There's never any cool water in the refrigerator.

Ne...que [▶25d] is not regarded as a negative in this context:

Nous n'avons que *de la* **bière.**	We have only beer.

When a negative does not relate to quantity, then indefinite and partitive forms are not reduced to **de**:

| Je n'ai pas *de* montre. | I don't have a watch. (*negative quantity*) |

But

| Ce n'est pas une montre. | This isn't a watch. (*negative identity*) |

(iv) **De** + adjective + noun

In most cases **des** should be reduced to **de** or **d'** when followed by adjective + noun.

| J'ai eu *de* gros problèmes. Est-ce qu'il y a *d'*autres questions? | I had major problems. Are there any other questions? |

However, this rule does not apply when adjective and noun are commonly used together in a particular combination:

| Tu peux acheter *des petits pois*? | Can you buy me some peas? |

19g   *Other indefinite determiners in French*

In addition to the use of the indefinite and partitive articles above [➤19e, 19f] the following forms should be noted:

(i)   **Aucun(e)** *(no, not any)* [➤25b (vi)]

| Il n'y a donc *aucun* problème, sauf peut-être pour choisir. | So there's *no* problem, except maybe in making a choice. |

(ii)   **Autre(s)** *(other)*

| Il y a une *autre* possibilité. Je peux proposer d'*autres* solutions. | There is *another* possibility. I can propose *other* solutions. |

(iii) *Chaque* (each, every)

Chaque exists only in this invariable singular form:

Chaque **établissement a son propre caractère.**	*Each* establishment has its own character.
Le menu est différent chaque **jour.**	The menu is different *every* day.

Note also the pronoun **chacun(e)**:

Chacune **de mes soeurs a participé à la cérémonie.**	*Each* of my sisters took part in the ceremony.

(iv) *Même(s)* (same)

Même is normally placed before the noun. It is more emphatic when placed after the noun:

Nous sommes arrivés par le *même* **train...**	We arrived by the *same* train . . .
...le jour *même* **où ils sont partis.**	. . . on the *very* day they left.

Le/la même, les mêmes can be used on their own, with the noun implied:

–**C'est ton ancien professeur?**	Is that your old teacher?
–**Oui, le** *même*.	Yes, the *very same*.

(v) *Plusieurs* (several)

Plusieurs exists only in this invariable plural:

Je connais *plusieurs* **endroits où on peut bien manger.**	I know *several* places where one can eat well.

(vi) *Quelque(s)* (some, a few)

Quelque in the singular is most frequently encountered in fixed expressions such as:

quelque chose   something   **quelque part**   somewhere

Other uses include:

Il habite à *quelque* distance d'ici.	He lives *some* distance from here.

In the plural, **quelques** means "some," "a few."

Nous avons invité *quelques* amis.	We've invited *a few* friends.
Il y a *quelques* restaurants dans les vieux quartiers.	There are *a few* restaurants in the old parts of the town.

 Quelquefois (sometimes) is written as one word.

(vii) *Tel, tels, telle, telles* (such)

Tel agrees with the noun it describes. It is normally placed before the noun:

Une *telle* histoire mérite notre attention.	*Such* a story warrants our attention.
De *tels* événements me semblent impensables.	*Such* events seem unthinkable to me.

It may also be used on its own, particularly in the construction **tel que:**

Elle était *telle que* je l'avais imaginée.	She was *as* I had imagined her to be.
Un port *tel que* Calais...	A port *such as* Calais . . .

 Tel cannot be used to qualify an adjective. In a phrase equivalent to "such a busy day," use **si**:

Une journée si occupée...	Such a busy day . . .

(viii) *Tout* (all, every)

The word **tout** has a range of uses in French. As an adjective it has the following forms:

	Singular	*Plural*
Masculine	**tout**	**tous**
Feminine	**toute**	**toutes**

It is normally followed by a definite article [➤19c] or a demonstrative [➤19d] or possessive [➤19h] determiner.

It has several equivalents in English, in which the article may or may not be present:

Il travaille *tout* le temps.	He works *all* the time.
***Tous* les soirs il reste au bureau...**	He stays in the office *every* evening . . .
...quelquefois *toute* la nuit.	. . . sometimes *all* night.
Son travail, c'est *toute* sa vie.	His work is his *whole* life.

The notion of 'every' can be expressed in two ways

tous les soirs	every evening
chaque soir	each, every evening

19h   *Belonging together: possessive determiners*

Possessives are used to show that the noun *belongs* to somebody or something. In French, they take their form from the *possessor* and their gender and number from the *thing possessed.* The words "belong" and "possessor" are used loosely here: possessives are also used for all sorts of other relationships between people and things.

The forms of the possessive are as follows:

(i)   Mon, ma, mes (my)

mon stylo	my pen	**mon** *before a masculine singular noun*
ma montre	my watch	**ma** *before a feminine singular noun*
mon ami(e)	my friend	**mon** *before any singular noun beginning with a vowel or mute* **h**
mes stylos	my pens	
mes montres	my watches	**mes** *before all plural nouns*
mes ami(e)s	my friends	

(ii)   *Ton, ta, tes* (your)

ton stylo	your pen	
ta montre	your watch	
ton ami(e)	your friend	*corresponds to* **tu** *form*
tes ami(e)s	your friends	

(iii)   *Son, sa, ses* (his, her, its)

son, sa, ses	his
son, sa, ses	her
son, sa, ses	its
son âge	his age, her age, its age
sa couleur	his color, her color, its color
ses qualités	his qualities, her qualities, its qualities

In the examples above, we cannot tell the gender of the *owner*, since the words appear in isolation. Generally, of course, the rest of the sentence gives us this information, as in the examples below:

La banque a fermé *ses* portes.	The bank has closed *its* doors.
***Son* directeur a été arrêté.**	*Its* director has been arrested.
***Sa* réputation est compromise.**	*His* reputation is ruined.
***Sa* femme l'a abandonné et elle vit maintenant avec sa fille.**	*His* wife has abandoned him and she is now living with her daughter.

In cases where it is necessary to identify the gender of the possessor, this can be done by the addition of the emphatic forms **à lui**, **à elle**:

C'est sa montre *à lui*.	It's *his* watch.
C'est son stylo *à elle*.	It's *her* pen.

(iv)   *Notre, nos* (our); *votre, vos* (your)

notre père	our father	**notre** *before masculine and feminine singular nouns*
notre mère	our mother	
nos fils	our sons	**nos** *before masculine and feminine plural nouns*
nos filles	our daughters	

votre père	your father	
votre mère	your mother	*corresponds to* **vous** *form*
vos fils	your sons	
vos filles	your daughters	

(v)   *Leur, leurs* (their)

leur père	their father		**leurs fils**	their sons
leur mère	their mother		**leurs filles**	their daughters

In cases where it is necessary to identify the gender of the possessor when using **leur(s)**, this can be done in French by adding the emphatic (disjunctive pronoun):

leur argent *à elles*	*their* money	*indicates that the owners are female*
leur argent *à eux*	*their* money	*indicates that the owners are male or male and female*

When referring to parts of the body, French often requires a definite article where in English a possessive determiner would be used [19c(iv)]:

Je me suis lavé les mains.	I washed my hands.

For possessive pronouns ➤21i.

20 Describing nouns: adjectives

20a What do adjectives do?

(i) Attributive and predicative adjectives

Adjectives describe nouns. They can be used either as part of a phrase containing a noun, that is, as *attributive* adjectives:

le *jeune* homme	the *young* man

or in the predicate of a sentence, that is, as *predicative* adjectives:

L'homme en question était *jeune*.	The man in question was *young*.

(ii) Agreement

Adjectives in French are singular or plural, masculine or feminine, according to the noun they relate to. While there are many variations in the ways in which feminine and plural forms are derived [➤20d, 20e] the basic pattern is that feminine forms add an **-e** while plural forms add **-s** (masculine) or **-es** (feminine):

	Singular	*Plural*
Masculine	le *petit* prince	les *petits* princes
Feminine	la *petite* princesse	les *petites* princesses

20b Accompanying the noun: attributive adjectives

(i) Position of adjectives

In French, adjectives normally follow the noun they relate to:

un passeport français	a French passport
un document confidentiel	a confidential document
une lettre désagréable	an unpleasant letter
une note excessive	an excessive bill

However, a number of common adjectives normally precede the noun:

beau	un beau jour d'été	a fine summer's day
bon	un bon repas	a good meal
grand	les grands concours	the big contests
gros	de gros problèmes	major problems
jeune	un jeune employé	a young employee
joli	une jolie plage	a pretty beach
long	un long discours	a long speech
mauvais	un mauvais début	a bad start
meilleur	un meilleur résultat	a better result
nouveau	un nouveau voisin	a new neighbor
petit	un petit conseil	a small piece of advice
vieux	les vieux arbres	the old trees

(ii) Even that great majority of adjectives which normally follow the noun can in certain circumstances precede it, particularly when used in a subjective or stylized way:

La Grèce et ses innombrables richesses...	Greece with its countless riches . . .
Les superbes sites historiques...	The superb historic sites . . .

(iii) A number of adjectives have a different meaning according to whether they precede or follow the noun:

ancien	un ancien collègue	a former colleague
	un bâtiment ancien	an ancient building
cher	mon cher ami	my dear friend
	une voiture chère	an expensive car
pauvre	ma pauvre chérie!	my poor darling! (pity)
	une famille pauvre	a poor family (money)
propre	leur propre maison	their own house
	une maison propre	a clean house
vrai	le vrai champagne	real champagne
	une histoire vraie	a true story

Nouns may also be followed by adjectival phrases [➤3c].

20c   *At a distance: predicative adjectives*

(i)   *Predicative* means "in the predicate" [➤4c]. These adjectives are usually the complement of the verb, that is, they are linked to the subject by a verb such as **être** (to be), **devenir** (to become), **sembler** (to seem).

Although separated from the noun they relate to, they nonetheless agree in number and gender exactly as when used attributively [➤20b]:

Les vins de Californie sont *intéressants*.	California wines are interesting.
La couleur de ce vin rouge me semble *bonne*.	The color of this red wine seems good to me.
Le bouquet est *agréable* **le goût est** *distingué* **et l'étiquette est** *jolie*!	The bouquet is pleasant, the taste is distinguished, and the label is pretty!

(ii) Agreement with more than one noun

When an adjective relates to two or more nouns, it is plural and agrees in gender:

La porte et la fenêtre sont ouvert*es*.	The door and the window are open.

If the nouns in the above example were of different genders, the adjective would be in the masculine plural:

La fenêtre et le volet sont ouvert*s*.	The window and the shutter are open.

(iii) Agreement with pronouns

Remember that pronouns such as **je, tu, nous, vous** may be feminine according to whom they refer to:

– Je suis prête, a dit Christine. Et toi, Philippe?	"I'm ready," said Christine. "Are you, Philippe?"
– Non, mais je serai prêt dans cinq minutes.	"No, but I will be in five minutes."
– Alors, nous ne serons pas les derniers.	"So we won't be the last."

(iv) Agreement with *on*

When the pronoun **on** is used instead of **nous**, it is followed by a plural adjectival agreement if the sense requires it [➤21b(iv)]:

| On ne sera pas les derniers. | We won't be the last. |

(v)   Agreement with **vous**

Vous can be singular or plural according to the context.

| **Vous êtes prêt?** | Are you ready? (*addressing one person*) |
| **Vous êtes prêts?** | Are you ready? (*more than one person*) |

(vi)   **Avoir chaud**, etc.

A number of everyday expressions which in English are rendered by "to be" + adjective are expressed in French using **avoir**, not **être**. They include:

avoir	**froid**	to be cold
avoir	**chaud**	to be warm, hot
avoir	**peur**	to be afraid
avoir	**mal**	to hurt, be in pain
avoir	**faim**	to be hungry
avoir	**soif**	to be thirsty
avoir	**tort**	to be wrong
avoir	**raison**	to be right
avoir	**sommeil**	to be sleepy
avoir	**honte**	to be ashamed

In these expressions, **chaud, froid**, etc. are invariable: no agreement is required.

| **Si les enfants ont soif, on peut boire quelque chose.** | If the children are thirsty, we can have a drink. |
| **Où est-ce que tu as mal? Partout!** | Where does it hurt? All over! |

[For **avoir** to express age ➤28d.]

20d   Feminine of adjectives

(i)   Ending **-e**

The basic pattern is that adjectives are made feminine by adding **-e**:

grand, grande   **vert, verte**

However, adjectives that already end in **-e** in the masculine form remain unchanged in the feminine:

un jeune homme   **une jeune femme**
un crayon rouge   **une cravate rouge**

(ii) *Other forms*

There are numerous cases where the feminine is not formed according to the above patterns. The most common are:

• Doubling of the final consonant + **e**:

bas	**basse**	low
épais	**épaisse**	thick
gras	**grasse**	fat
gros	**grosse**	big
gentil	**gentille**	nice
bon	**bonne**	good
cruel	**cruelle**	cruel
italien	**italienne**	Italian
muet	**muette**	dumb
pareil	**pareille**	alike

• Masculine in **-c**, feminine in **-che**:

blanc	**blanche**	white
franc	**franche**	frank
sec	**sèche**	dry (*note grave accent*)

• Masculine in **-x**, feminine in **-se**:

heureux	**heureuse**	happy
jaloux	**jalouse**	jealous

Exceptions:

roux	**rousse**	redheaded
doux	**douce**	gentle
faux	**fausse**	false

• Masculine in **-er, -ier,** feminine in **-ère, -ière**:

léger	**légère**	light
premier	**première**	first

• Masculine in **-f**, feminine in **-ve**:

vif	**vive**	lively
naïf	**naïve**	naive

• Masculine in **-eau**, feminine in **-elle**;
• Masculine in **-ou**, feminine in **-olle**:

beau	**belle**	fine, handsome, beautiful
nouveau	**nouvelle**	new
fou	**folle**	mad
mou	**molle**	soft

This group of adjectives has a second masculine singular form **bel, nouvel, fol, mol**, which must be used before a noun beginning with a vowel or mute **h**.

 Vieux (vieil), vieille (old) has the same features: for example, **vieil hibou**.

20e Plural of adjectives

(i) Feminine plural

The plural of *all adjectives in the feminine* is formed by adding **-s** to the feminine singular. This holds true for both regular and irregular forms:

blanche	**blanches**
vieille	**vieilles**

(ii) Masculine plural

Most adjectives form their *masculine plural* by adding **-s** to the masculine singular form, but there are a number of exceptions, closely mirroring the formation of plural nouns [▶18e]:

Masculine singular	*Masculine plural*	
-eau	**-eaux**	**beau, beaux**
-s, -x	*unchanged*	**gros, faux**
-al	**aux**	**primordial, primordiaux**

Exceptions: **fatals, finals, banals, navals**.

20f Invariable adjectives

A very small number of adjectives are unchanged in the feminine and plural. They include borrowings from English (e.g., **snob**, snobbish), colors in compound forms (**gris-bleu**, blue-gray; **vert clair**, light green; **bleu foncé**, dark blue) and a few single colors (**marron**, brown; **khaki**, khaki; **or**, gold; **châtain**, chestnut).

Adjectives may be used as nouns [➤18f].

20g   *More and most: comparative and superlative*

(i)   *Comparisons*

Most (though not all) adjectives can be used to make comparisons. For this we use either the *comparative* or the *superlative* form:

Marie-Christine a douze ans.	Marie-Christine is twelve years old.
Josiane est *plus jeune*, elle a dix ans.	Josiane is *younger* – she is ten.
Christel a sept ans: elle est *la plus jeune* et *la plus bavarde*.	Christel is seven: she is *the youngest* – and *the most talkative*.

In English there are two ways of producing comparatives and superlatives: either by adding *-er* and *-est* (mainly to short words such as *long*, to form *longer*, *longest*) or by the insertion of the words *more*, *most*, as in *more difficult*, *most difficult*.

(ii)   *Formation*

In French there is a single basic method for deriving comparative and superlative forms, the insertion of the word **plus** to form comparatives and **le/la/les plus** to form superlatives. When the adjective accompanies the noun, the comparative or superlative takes the same position as the basic adjective, before or after the noun:

une vieille rue	an old street
une plus vieille rue	an older street
la plus vieille rue	the oldest street
une rue intéressante	an interesting street
une rue plus intéressante	a more interesting street
la rue la plus intéressante	the most interesting street

Notice that where the superlative form follows the noun, the article is repeated, using the same number and gender:

les endroits les plus dangereux	the most dangerous places

(iii)   *With possessive determiners (**mon**, **ma**, **mes**, etc)*

Where a possessive determiner (**mon, ma, mes; ton, ta, tes**, etc.) is used, it replaces the article introducing the superlative, in cases where the adjective precedes the noun. Where the adjective follows the noun, the article introducing the superlative is unaffected:

son *plus gros* paquet	his/her *largest* parcel
son paquet *le plus lourd*	his/her *heaviest* parcel

(iv) Bon, mauvais

The adjectives **bon** and **mauvais** have irregular forms of the comparative and superlative.

bon	good	**une bonne nouvelle**	good news
meilleur	better	**une meilleure nouvelle**	better news
le meilleur	best	**la meilleure nouvelle**	the best news
mauvais	bad	**un mauvais rêve**	a bad dream
pire *or*			
plus mauvais	worse	**un plus mauvais jour**	a worse day
le pire *or* **le plus**			
mauvais	worst	**le plus mauvais temps**	the worst weather

The forms **pire** and **le pire** are nowadays restricted in use to predicative constructions [►20c], and then only in generalized emotional or moral reactions:

La situation aujourd'hui est *pire* **que jamais.**	The situation today is worse than ever.

Note also **moindre** (lesser, smaller); **le moindre** (least, smallest):

Tu m'appelleras si tu as *le moindre* **problème.**	You will call me if you have the least (smallest) problem.

However, *small*, *smaller*, *smallest*, when comparing size, would normally be expressed by the adjective **petit**:

Cueille les meilleurs fruits, et laisse *les plus petits*.	Pick the best fruit, and leave *the smallest.*

(v) Plus...que (more ... than)

Catherine est *plus* **grande** *que* **son frère.**	Catherine is taller than her brother.

| La vieille ville est *plus* pittoresque *que* les quartiers modernes. | The old town is more picturesque than the modern districts. |

(vi) Moins (less, least)

The comparative and superlative forms introduced by **moins** (less, least) instead of **plus**, follow exactly the same patterns of formation and use:

| Le théâtre serait *moins* cher *que* l'opéra.
Le cinéma serait *moins* cher *que* le théâtre.
Oui, c'est le cinéma qui serait *le moins* cher. Allons-y! | The theater would be less expensive than the opera.
The movies would be less expensive than the theater.
Yes, the movies would be the least expensive. Let's go! |

(vii) Other expressions

In addition to comparisons involving **plus ... que** and **moins ... que**, the following similar expressions are useful:

aussi...que   as . . . as

| Notre jardin est *aussi* négligé *que* celui des voisins. | Our yard is *as* neglected *as* the neighbors'. |

pas si (or pas aussi)...que   not as . . . as

| Edwige n'est *pas (aus)si* grande *que* sa sœur. | Edwige is *not as* tall *as* her sister. |

(viii)

Note the use of **de** after superlatives, where in English the words "in" or "on" would be used:

| Le magasin le plus cher *de* la rue. | The most expensive department store *on* the street. |

[For **plus de** and **moins de** as expressions of quantity ➤19f. The subjunctive is used after superlatives in certain situations ➤14e(ii). For comparative and superlative forms of adverbs ➤24b(iii)].

21 Representing nouns: pronouns

21a What pronouns do

(i) Use

The word *pronoun* means "in place of a noun." We constantly use pronouns instead of nouns, as a way of avoiding repetition:

J'ai un nouveau voisin, Georges Lemaître. *Il* est plombier. Je *l'*ai rencontré pour la première fois quand *lui* et sa femme sont passés nous dire bonjour dimanche dernier. Je *lui* ai prêté ma tondeuse parce que *la sienne* était en panne.	I have a new neighbor, Georges Lemaître. *He*'s a plumber. I met *him* for the first time when *he* and his wife called to say hello last Sunday. I lent *him* my lawn mower because *his* had broken down.

(ii) Form

All pronouns in French:

• Take their gender (masculine/feminine) and their number (singular/plural) from the noun they refer to;
• Take their form from their function in the sentence.

(iii) Personal pronouns

Personal pronouns are the most neutral pronouns – they simply replace nouns without adding further information. They may refer to the person(s) speaking (first person), the person(s) spoken to (second person), or the person(s) or thing(s) spoken about (third person).

21b Personal pronouns

(i) Subject pronouns

The subject pronouns are:

	Singular		Plural	
First person	**je**	I	**nous**	we
Second person	**tu**	you	**vous**	you

Third person	**il**	he, it	**ils**	they
	elle	she, it	**elles**	they

(ii) Use

(A) Je becomes **j'** before a vowel or mute **h**:

J'habite Douai, j'ai un appartement dans le centre.	I live in Douai: I have an apartment in the town center.

(B) Tu is used when addressing family, close friends, and children, and is a mark of closeness or familiarity. Young people, especially students, increasingly use **tu** to their peers, whether or not they are in the familiar category. In other situations, for example, with other acquaintances or with strangers, the **vous** form is generally used. Note that while **tu** can only be used as a singular form, **vous** can be singular or plural:

Tu n'as pas froid, Christine?	You're not cold, are you, Christine?
Vous n'avez pas froid, madame?	You're not cold, are you, Madam? (*singular, formal*)
Vous n'avez pas froid, mes enfants?	You're not cold, are you, children? (*plural, informal*)
Vous n'avez pas froid, mesdames?	You're not cold, are you, ladies? (*plural, formal*)

 The line between familiarity and formality varies between countries and languages. In this respect French is more formal than English. Except among young people, it is wise therefore for visitors to France to use **vous** with adults unless invited to do otherwise.

 Tu can be used deliberately as a sign of contempt, in situations where normally the **vous** form would be expected.

(C) Ils is used when referring to masculine nouns in the plural, or to a mixture of masculine and feminine nouns. **Elles** is used to refer to feminine nouns in the plural:

As-tu vu Brigitte et Paul? Oui, *ils* sont partis à la piscine.	Have you seen Brigitte and Paul? Yes, *they* have gone off to the swimmimg pool.
Mais *ils* ont oublié leurs serviettes. *Elles* sont là sur la table.	But *they've* forgotten their towels. *They* are here on the table.

(D) Where two subject pronouns are used together before a verb, the emphatic forms are required [➤21f]:

Toi et *moi*, **nous allons travailler ensemble.**	*You* and *I* are going to work together.
Vous et *elle*, **vous êtes ensemble?**	Are *you* and *she* together?

(iii)   The indefinite pronoun *on*

The subject pronoun **on** is known as an indefinite pronoun since it is frequently used to make statements about no one in particular:

On **peut très facilement faire ce genre d'erreur.**	One can very easily make this sort of mistake.

 Do not confuse **on** with **un/une** used as a number in:

Un **de mes enfants me l'a dit.**	One of my children told me.

(iv)   Uses of *on*

In French, **on** is much more widely used than "one" in English. Often, it has no direct correspondence in English, as in these instances:

(A) Where a passive form would normally be used in English, by making an indirect object become the subject of a passive construction. This is not possible in French, which therefore uses **on** as a way of avoiding specifying who did the action [➤15 for the use of the passive]:

On **m'a recommandé un nouveau restaurant japonais.**	A new Japanese restaurant has been recommended to me.

(B) In speech, where it is very commonly used to replace **nous**:

Alors, ce soir, *on* **va au restaurant ou** *on* **reste à la maison?**	So are we going out to the restaurant this evening, or staying at home?

When **on** is used instead of **nous**, it is common (though not obligatory) for agreements to be made to match the implied **nous**:

On **est bête(s), toi et moi, d'avoir peur de manger des choses exotiques.**	It is foolish of us to be scared of eating anything exotic.

(C) Instead of **ils**, to convey a generalized "they":

On **dit que les Japonais mangent plus sainement que nous.**	They say the Japanese eat more healthily than we do.

(D) Quelqu'un (someone) and **n'importe qui** (anyone [at all]) are also used as indefinite forms:

Quelqu'un **a sonné il y a cinq minutes.**	Someone rang the doorbell five minutes ago.
N'importe qui **peut pénétrer dans la maison si tu ne fermes pas la porte.**	Anyone can get into the house if you don't close the door.

(iv)   *Object pronouns*

There are three types of object pronoun: direct, indirect, and reflexive. The three types are identical in the first- and second-person forms, both singular and plural. The third-person forms are different in each case.

• The direct object pronouns are:

	Singular		Plural	
First person	**me**	me	**nous**	us
Second person	**te**	you	**vous**	you
Third person	**le**	him, it	**les**	them
	la	her, it	**les**	them

• The indirect object pronouns are:

First person	**me**	to me	**nous**	to us
Second person	**te**	to you	**vous**	to you
Third person	**lui**	to him, to her, to it	**leur**	to them

NOUNS AND NOUN PHRASES

In English the distinction between direct and indirect objects is often blurred by the omission of the word "to," as in the following example:

I will send him a reply next week.

In the above example the direct object is "reply," and the indirect object is "him." You can easily check if a noun or pronoun is a direct or indirect object: if you can use the word "to" before the object without making nonsense of the sentence, the object is indirect:

Je *lui* enverrai une réponse la semaine prochaine.	I will send a reply *(to)* him next week.

but in the following example, adding "to" would not work – "him" is a direct object:

Je *l'*enverrai voir un spécialiste la semaine prochaine.	I will send *him* to see a specialist next week.

(v) *Reflexive pronouns*

Reflexive pronouns are object pronouns that refer back to the subject of the sentence, as when you do something to yourself. They have the same form whether they serve as direct or indirect object pronouns:

	Singular		**Plural**
me	(to) myself	**nous**	(to) ourselves
te	(to) yourself	**vous**	(to) yourself/yourselves
se	(to) himself, herself, itself	**se**	(to) themselves

• Reflexive verb constructions in French sometimes have directly equivalent forms in English:

Il *s'*est blessé en jouant au tennis.	He injured *himself* playing tennis.
Je *me* suis promis de ne pas prendre les mêmes risques.	I promised *myself* not to take the same risks.

• Sometimes, however, the English equivalents have no obvious *reflexive* value, for example:

Il *se* gratte l'oreille.	He scratches his ear.
Elle *se* ronge les ongles.	She bites her nails.
Je *me* souviens de ce programme.	I remember that program.
Elle *s'*en va.	She goes away. (**s'en aller**, to go away)

• Reflexive forms are also used in the plural to convey the idea of "(to) each other/one another":

Ils ne se parlent plus.	They no longer speak to each other.
Les enfants se téléphonent souvent.	The children often telephone one another.

[For further information on reflexive verbs ►8c, 11c].

 The pronouns **me, te, le, la, se** become **m', t', l', s'** before a vowel or mute **h**.

(vi) *Position of object pronouns*

With all forms of the verb, except some imperatives [►(viii)b, below] and some uses of **faire** and **laisser** [►9f], object pronouns are placed immediately before the verb of which they are the object:

Je cherche les romans policiers.	I'm looking for detective stories.
Où est-ce que je *les* trouverai?	Where will I find *them*?
Ils sont au premier étage. Vous allez *les* trouver à votre gauche.	They are on the first floor. You will find *them* on your left.

In compound tense forms the object pronoun comes before the auxiliary verb:

Les romans d'Agatha Christie, je *les* ai tous lus.	As for Agatha Christie's novels, I've read them all.

In negative sentences, the **ne** comes before the object pronoun:

...mais je *ne les* ai pas relus récemment.	. . . but I haven't reread them lately.

(vii)   Order of object pronouns

(A) When two object pronouns occur together they follow this order:

me				
te	le			
se	la	lui		
nous	les	leur	y	en
vous				

Il me la présente.	He presents it to me.
Je la lui rends.	I give it back to him.

(B) With imperative forms, the position, form, and order of object pronouns depend on whether the imperative is positive or negative. With negative imperatives, the position, form, and order are as set out as in **(A)** above:

Ne me l'envoyez pas.	Don't send it to me.

With positive imperative forms, object pronouns:

- are placed after the verb;
- follow a different order;
- in some cases have a different form;
- are hyphenated except after **m'** and **t'**.

See the table below:

	moi, m'		
	toi, t'		
le	lui	y	en
la	nous		
les	vous		
	leur		

Envoyez-les-lui.	Send them to him.	**Envoyez-m'en.**	Send me some.

21c   The pronoun y

(i)   *Y*, meaning "there"

The pronoun **y** can be used to replace any preposition indicating location, such as **à**, **dans**, **sur**, **devant**, **sous**, **à côté de** +

noun. When used in this way, it has a generalized meaning "there," as in the following illustrations:

Je vous retrouve devant la station de métro à huit heures?	Shall I meet you outside the subway at eight o'clock?
Oui, j'y serai.	Yes, I'll be there.
J'avais laissé le journal sur cette chaise, mais il n'y est plus.	I had left the newspaper on this chair, but it isn't there any more.
As-tu regardé dans la cuisine?	Have you looked in the kitchen?
Je crois qu'il y est.	I think it's in there.

As the above examples show, **y** will sometimes be translated by "to it" or "in it," but frequently also by "there" in English.

Note that very often no word for **y** is present in English:

Vous allez à la plage cette semaine?	Are you going to the beach this week?
Oui, nous y allons demain.	Yes we are going tomorrow.

(ii) **Y** *replaces* **à**

The pronoun **y** replaces **à** even when **à** does not refer to a location, for example, in expressions like **penser à** (to think about). However, when used in this way, **y** can only refer to a thing or things, never to people:

Je pense à mes vacances. J'y pense souvent!	I'm thinking about my vacations. I often think about *them!*

but

Je pense à mes parents. Je pense souvent à *eux*.	I'm thinking about my parents. I often think about *them*.

[For more detail ➤21f.]

(iii) **Y** *replaces* **à** *+ infinitive*

Many French verbs are linked to following infinitives by **à**. In such cases, **y** can be used to replace the infinitive, as in these examples:

NOUNS AND NOUN PHRASES

arriver à faire quelque chose	manage to do something
renoncer à faire quelque chose	to give up doing something

Après beaucoup d'effort, j'y suis arrivé.	After a lot of effort I managed it.
J'ai renoncé à fumer. J'y renonce au moins une fois par mois.	I've given up smoking. I give up at least once a month.

(iv)   Position

Y follows the rules relating to object pronouns in terms of position [➤21b(vii)]:

En trouvant nos places, nous nous y sommes installés.	Once we found our seats, we took our places.

Note the following useful imperative forms:

Allez-y, vas-y!	Go on! (*used for any sort of encouragement*)
Allons-y!	Let's go! (*used only for going somewhere*)

21d   The pronoun en

(i)   En replaces de

The prononun **en** replaces **de** (or one of its forms) + a noun. Given the range of uses of **de** in French, **en** covers a wide range of meanings in English.

As-tu de l'argent allemand pour notre voyage? Oui, j'en ai (j'ai de l'argent).	Have you any German money for our trip? Yes I have (some).
Tu as donc été à la banque? Oui, j'en reviens (je reviens de la banque).	So you've been to the bank? Yes, I've just come back (from there).
Et est-ce que tu as pris aussi de la monnaie belge? Non, je n'en ai pas pris.	And did you get some Belgian currency as well? No, I didn't (get any).
Mais je t'en avais parlé hier soir!	But I talked to you about it last night!

(ii)   *With expressions of quantity*

En often appears with expressions of quantity, since these are generally followed by **de**.

Tu as des problèmes en ce moment? Oui, j'*en* ai trop (j'ai trop de problèmes).	Do you have problems at the moment? Yes, I have too many (of them).
J'*en* ai deux en particulier si tu as le temps de me donner ton opinion.	I have two (of them) in particular if you have time to give me your opinion.

As the above examples illustrate, **en** is required in French where in many cases in English its equivalent is absent or understood.

(iii)   *Position*

Like **y**, **en** follows the same rules of position as the object pronouns [➤21b(vii)]:

Tu lui *en* as parlé hier?	Did you talk to him about it yesterday?
Envoyez-nous-*en* le plus tôt possible.	Send us some as soon as possible.

(iv)   *Antecedent*

Like **y**, **en** is normally only used to refer to things, not people:

Mon travail? J'*en* parle souvent.	My work? I often talk *about it.*
Ma fille? Je parle souvent d'elle.	My daughter? I often talk *about her.*

The word **en** exists also as a very common preposition [➤23b(xiii)].

21e   Impersonal pronouns

The subject pronoun **il** and the object pronoun **le** are frequently used impersonally in French (as in English) to convey a non-specific "it."

(i)   *Use of il*

Il is used:

• as the subject of a number of fixed impersonal verbs;
• to introduce statements about the weather, time, etc.;

• to anticipate the true subject of a sentence;
• occasionally with verbs that are not invariably impersonal.

(A) Il is used as the subject of fixed impersonal verbs, such as **il y a** (there is, there are), **il faut** (it is necessary), **il s'agit de** (it is a matter of):

Il y a des choses intéressantes à la télévision ce soir?	Is there anything interesting on television this evening?
Oui, il faut absolument qu'on regarde l'entretien avec le ministre de l'éducation.	Yes, we must watch the interview with the minister of education.
Il s'agit de la réforme du primaire.	It's about reform of the primary schools.

(B) Il is used to introduce statements about the weather, time, etc.:

Il est quelle heure?	What is the time?
Il est sept heures et demie.	It's half past seven.
Tu as regardé la météo? Tu sais quel temps il va faire demain?	Did you watch the weather forecast? Do you know what the weather is going to be tomorrow?
Apparemment, il va pleuvoir; il fait déjà très sombre.	Apparently it's going to rain. It's already gloomy.

(ii) *The weather: Il fait . . .*

The following list of weather terms shows the use of the impersonal **il**:

Il fait beau.	It is fine and sunny.
Il fait sec.	It is dry.
Il fait sombre/gris.	It is gloomy, overcast.
Il fait du soleil.	It is sunny.
Il fait un temps couvert.	It is overcast.
Il fait un temps orageux.	It is thundery.
Il fait lourd.	It is humid.
Il fait du brouillard.	It is foggy.
Il fait du vent.	It is windy.
Il fait froid.	It is cold.
Il fait chaud.	It is warm/hot.
Il fait doux.	It is mild.
Il fait humide.	It is wet, damp.

Note also:

Il fait nuit.	It is dark (night).
Il fait noir.	It is dark (e.g., *in a tunnel*).
Il fait jour.	It is daylight.
Il fait clair.	It is light (e.g., *of a room*).
Il pleut.	It is raining.
Il neige.	It is snowing.
Il grêle.	It is hailing.
Il gèle.	It is freezing.

(iii) **Il** is used to anticipate the true subject of a sentence, very often in the interest of balance or emphasis:

Alors il sera difficile de faire un pique-nique (faire un pique-nique sera difficile).	So it will be difficult to have a picnic.
Il reste une heure avant les informations.	There is another hour before the news.

(iv)   *Le, l'*

The pronoun **le/l'** is used as an object or complement as a means of referring back to a statement or fact:

Jacqueline Martin était speakerine, mais elle ne l'est plus.	Jacqueline Martin used to be a TV announcer, but she isn't any more.
Mais je te l'ai dit hier.	But I told you (so) yesterday.

More often than not the nearest equivalent in English is "so," as in the above example. Care is needed to avoid confusion with other equivalents of the English "so," as in:

Ils sont si riches.	They are so rich.
Vous êtes donc venus.	So you came.

21f   *Disjunctive pronouns*

The personal subject and object pronouns described in the preceding sections [▶21b–21e] are all unstressed in French, that is, they cannot be used in isolation from the verb or in an emphatic position. Wherever such isolation or emphasis occurs, a pronoun form known as the disjunctive pronoun is used. In English there are no separate disjunctive pronouns, as ordinary subject and object forms are employed.

(i) *The disjunctive pronouns:*

moi	me	**nous**	us
toi	you	**vous**	you
lui	him	**eux**	them (*masculine, or masc/fem mix*)
elle	her	**elles**	them (*feminine*)

There is an additional disjunctive pronoun, **soi**, corresponding to the subject pronoun **on** [➤21b(iv)].

Disjunctive forms are used only for pronouns referring to people.

(ii) *Uses*

The following are typical uses:

(A) Disjunctive forms are used whenever the pronoun stands alone or is introduced by **c'est** or one of its forms:

Qui est responsable?	Who is responsible?
Elle (*or* **C'est elle).**	She is
Vous, ici?	What are *you* doing here?

(B) Disjunctive forms are used to give more emphasis to a pronoun in speech (bearing in mind that one cannot in French pronounce ordinary pronouns like **je** or **il** emphatically).

Je ne sais pas, moi.	*I* don't know.
Je ne peux pas les supporter, eux.	I can't stand *them*.

(C) Disjunctive pronouns are used after prepositions, since the effect of a preposition is to throw into relief the word following it:

Viens avec moi.	Come with me.
Tu vois le vieux monsieur en face de nous? C'est chez lui que nous allons prendre l'apéritif demain soir.	Do you see the old gentleman opposite us? We're going to his house for drinks tomorrow evening.

(D) Disjunctive pronouns are used after the preposition **à** to convey possession:

Ce bouquin est à toi?	Is this book yours?
Oui, il est à moi.	Yes, it's mine.

Note also the frequent use of **à** + a disjunctive pronoun or noun to convey the idea of responsibility, obligation, or role:

C'est à nous de payer.	We're the ones who have to pay.
C'est à lui de surveiller les travaux.	It's his job to oversee the work.

(E) Disjunctive pronouns are used after **que** in comparatives:

Il est plus malin que moi...	He is craftier than I am . . .
...mais moi, je suis plus patient que lui.	. . . but I'm more patient than he is.

(F) Disjunctive pronouns are also used where more than one pronoun is specified as the subject or object of a verb:

Toi et moi, nous allons travailler ensemble.	You and I are going to work together.
Lui et elle, ils sont partis hier.	He and she left yesterday.
Je les ai vus, lui et elle.	I saw him and her.

(G) Disjunctive pronouns are used with words like **aussi**, **surtout**, and **seul** for emphasis:

Lui seul est resté au bureau.	He alone stayed in the office.
Lui surtout a besoin de repos.	He above all needs rest.
Moi aussi, je suis fatigué.	I'm tired as well.

Note from the above examples that while it is possible for the third-person disjunctive pronoun to stand alone as the subject, in the first-person singular the **je** cannot be omitted.

(H) Disjunctive pronouns plus **-même(s)** are used to convey the emphatic forms "myself," "yourself," etc.

moi-même	myself	**nous-mêmes**	ourselves
toi-même	yourself	**vous-même(s)**	yourself, yourselves

lui-même	himself	**eux-mêmes**	themselves
elle-même	herself	**elles-mêmes**	themselves
			(*feminine*)
soi-même	oneself		

J'ai lavé la voiture moi-même.	I washed the car myself.
Tu m'as vu toi-même.	You yourself saw me.

 Be careful not to confuse the emphatic use of **moi-même**, etc., with the use of reflexive pronouns [➤21b(vi)]:

Je me suis lavé.	I washed myself. (*"myself" is the object of "washed"*)
J'ai lavé la voiture moi-même.	I washed the car myself. (*"myself" emphasizes "I"; "car" is the object*)

(I) **Moi** and **toi** are used after positive imperative forms [➤21b(vii)]:

Donnez-le-moi!	Give it to me!

21g   *Interrogative pronouns*

(i)   The interrogative pronouns are used to ask the following sorts of question:

Qui est ce jeune homme?	Who is that young man?
C'est un des copains de Sophie.	It's one of Sophie's boyfriends.
Que penses-tu de lui?	What do you think of him?
Il est gentil.	He's nice.
J'ai vu l'autre copain de Sophie.	I've seen Sophie's other boyfriend.
Lequel préfères-tu?	Which one do you prefer?

 The pronouns **qui** and **que** both have other uses in French. It is particularly easy to confuse their use here with their use as relative pronouns [➤21j]. Similarly, in English *who* and *which* also double as relative pronouns, while *what* and *which* serve also as interrogative determiners. Here are some contrasted examples to help show the distinctions:

Le jeune homme qui vient de téléphoner demandait à parler à Sophie.	The young man who has just telephoned was asking to speak to Sophie. (*relative pronoun*)
C'était quel copain?	Which boyfriend was it? (*interrogative determiner*)
C'est le jeune homme que tu m'as indiqué hier.	He is the young man (whom) you pointed out to me yesterday. (relative pronoun)
Quelle réponse dois-je donner s'il rappelle?	What reply must I give if he calls again? (interrogative determiner)

(ii) *People:* ***Qui? Qui est-ce qui/que...?*** *Who?*

(A) When used as a subject pronoun, **Qui?** or **Qui est-ce qui?** means *who?*

Qui aime rencontrer des gens? Qui est-ce qui aime rencontrer des gens?	Who likes meeting people?

The longer form is largely restricted to speech.

(B) When used as an object pronoun, **Qui?** or **Qui est-ce que...?** means *whom?*

Qui rencontrez-vous au cours de votre travail? Qui est-ce que vous rencontrez au cours de votre travail?	Whom do you meet in the course of your work?

(*Whom* is now largely restricted to formal language in English. Its inclusion here can, however, be helpful in distinguishing subject and object forms in French.)

 When using **Qui est-ce que...?** the **que** changes to **qu'** before a vowel. **Qui** does not change:

Qui est-ce qu'on a invité?	Who have we invited?

(C) After a preposition the form is **Qui?** or **Qui est-ce que/qu'...?**

Avec qui vient-il?   With whom is he coming?
Avec qui est-ce qu'il vient?

The longer form is largely restricted to speech.

 To say "With whom is he coming?" sounds somewhat stilted and old-fashioned in English, but provides a reminder that in French the preposition cannot be placed at the end of a sentence, as in colloquial English, "Who is he coming with?" The only concession in French is that the preposition + pronoun are frequently moved together to the end in current speech:

Il vient avec qui?   Who is he coming with?

Note also the useful question:

A qui est ce chapeau?   Whose is this hat?
Il est à moi.   It's mine.

(iii)   Things: *Que? Qu'est-ce que...?*

(A) When used as a subject pronoun, the only interrogative form for *what?* is **Qu'est-ce qui...?** No alternative form exists.

Qu'est-ce qui donne le meilleur   What gives the best result?
résultat?

(B) When used as an object pronoun **Que...?** and **Qu'est-ce que...?** mean *what?*

Que fais-tu?   What are you doing?
Qu'est-ce que tu fais?

In both cases, **que** changes to **qu'** before a vowel:

Qu'as-tu fait?   What have you done? What did
                                       you do?
Qu'est-ce qu'ils ont fait?   What have they done? What did
                                       they do?

(C) After a preposition *what* is **quoi**:

Avec quoi vas-tu écrire?	What are you going to write with? (With what . . .)

(iv)   *Interrogative pronouns in indirect speech*

(A) When referring to people, the interrogative pronoun in indirect speech [➤5c, 5d] is always **qui**:

Je ne sais pas qui sera là ce soir.	I don't know who will be there this evening. (*subject*)
J'allais vous demander qui on verra.	I was going to ask you who we will see. (*object*)
Je me demande avec qui Louise viendra.	I wonder who Louise will come with? (with whom Louise will come) (*after preposition*)

(B) When referring to things, the interrogative pronoun in indirect speech varies according to whether the pronoun is subject or object of the clause it is in, or is after a preposition:

Je ne sais pas *ce qui* inquiète ma mère.	I don't know what is worrying my mother. (*subject of* **inquiète**)
Je lui ai demandé *ce qu'*elle veut faire.	I've asked her what she wants to do. (*object of* **faire**)
Tu peux lui demander *de quoi* elle a peur?	Can you ask her what she is afraid of? (of what she is afraid?) (*after preposition*)

(v)   *The interrogative pronoun **lequel***

Lequel? as an interrogative pronoun means *which one?* (people or things). Its forms are those of the two words which make it up, **le** and **quel**:

	Singular	*Plural*
Masculine	**lequel**	**lesquels**
Feminine	**laquelle**	**lesquelles**

Alors, tu as choisi ta cravate? Laquelle vas-tu mettre?	So have you chosen your tie? Which one are you going to put on?
Moi, je ne sais pas quelles chaussures porter. Lesquelles me vont mieux?	Personally I don't know which shoes to wear. Which ones suit me best?

The same forms are used in indirect speech:

Ne me demande pas lesquelles je préfère, je suis très mauvais juge.	Don't ask me which ones I prefer – I'm a very bad judge.

• **Lequel** combines with the prepositions **à** and **de** to form the following:

	Singular		*Plural*	
Masculine	**auquel**	**duquel**	**auxquels**	**desquels**
Feminine	**à laquelle**	**de laquelle**	**auxquelles**	**desquelles**

Elles sont trois sœurs. Tu parles de laquelle?	There are three sisters. Which one are you talking about?

➤ [For interrogative determiner **quel** ➤19b; for **lequel** as a relative pronoun ➤21j].

21h   *Pointing and showing: demonstrative pronouns*

Demonstrative pronouns are used to point out or emphasize things – the equivalent in English being "this one," "that one," "these/those (ones)." They are often used to convey whether something is near to or far from the speaker, though sometimes this distance is mental rather than physical.

(i)   *Forms*

In French the demonstrative pronoun forms are:

	Masculine	*Feminine*
Singular	**celui**	**celle**
Plural	**ceux**	**celles**

The above forms have the same number and gender as the noun they stand for.

The forms of **celui** cannot stand alone. They are always followed by either the demonstrative suffix (**-ci/-là**), a relative pronoun (**qui, que, dont**), or a preposition (generally **de**).

(ii) *Celui-ci, celui-là*

This form is used where the need is to point out and to differentiate:

Celui-ci **coûte moins cher que** *celui-là*.	This one costs less than that one.
Des deux voitures, je préfère *celle-là* **parce qu'elle a le toit ouvrant.**	Of the two cars I prefer that one/this one because it has a sunroof.

 There is not an exact match between **-ci/-là** in French and "this/that" in English, since **-là** is more widely used in French as a general pointer meaning both "this" and "that," "here" and "there." It is better to think in terms of the notions of contrast and emphasis rather than a direct word equivalent in English. This also explains why these forms are used to convey an idea that in English can only be rendered by the rather formal construction "former/latter."

J'avais écrit à mon père et à mon frère.	I had written to my father and my brother.
Celui-ci **m'a répondu le premier.**	It was the latter who replied first.

 -ci/-là can be added to nouns as well as the pronoun **celui** [➤19d]:

Je préfère cette voiture-*ci*.	I prefer this car.

(iii) *Celui* + *relative pronoun*

Celui can be followed by **qui** (subject), **que** (object) or a preposition + **qui/que**. Don't forget that **de** + relative **qui** is expressed by **dont** [➤21j, relative pronouns].

Prends une veste – celle que je t'ai sortie.	Take a jacket – the one I've taken out for you. (**que** *object of* **j'ai sortie**)

Celle qui est sur le lit?	The one (which is) on the bed? (**qui** *subject of* **est**)
Oui, celle dont j'ai réparé la poche hier.	Yes, the one I repaired the pocket of yesterday. (*of which I repaired the pocket*)

Ceux can also be used as "those who," "the people who."

Ceux qui préfèrent aller à la piscine, levez la main!	Hands up, those who prefer to go swimming!
Tous ceux que j'ai rencontrés m'ont dit la même chose.	Everyone I met said the same thing.

(iv) **Celui** *+ preposition*

In the majority of cases the preposition after **celui** is **de**:

J'avais perdu mon parapluie, alors j'ai pris celui de mon mari.	I had lost my umbrella, so I took my husband's (that of my husband).
J'ai un agenda mais c'est celui de l'an dernier.	I have a diary but it's last year's.

It is particularly important to note in these examples that **celui** + **de** is more often than not rendered in English by a possessive with apostrophe *'s*.

(v) **Cela, ça, ceci**

Whereas **celui** in its various forms means "this one," "that one," the pronouns **cela**, **ça**, and **ceci** mean simply "this" and "that" and carry no gender or number because they never refer to a named person or thing. **Ça** is a colloquial form of **cela**.

Regarde ceci.	Look at this.
Cela/ça te semble raisonnable?	Does that seem reasonable to you?

Shopkeepers frequently use the following question:

Et avec ceci?	What else can I get you?

The following question, frequently heard in conversation, is used when seeking to identify something:

Qu'est-ce que c'est que ça/cela?   What's that?

 The question in English *Who's that?* is rendered in French using the pronoun **ce**:

Qui est-ce?   Who is it?/Who is that?

21i Belonging together: possessive pronouns

Possessive pronouns are unique in that they represent two different nouns at once: the *possessor* and the *thing possessed*. Like possessive determiners [➤19h] they take their form from the possessor, and their gender and number from the thing possessed.

The forms of the possessive pronoun are:

le mien	la mienne	les miens	les miennes	mine
le tien	la tienne	les tiens	les tiennes	yours
le sien	la sienne	les siens	les siennes	his, hers
le nôtre	la nôtre	les nôtres		ours
le vôtre	la vôtre	les vôtres		yours
le leur	la leur	les leurs		theirs

Here are some examples of the possessive pronoun in use:

Hélène, tu as nos passeports?   Hélène, have you got our passports?

Oui, le mien est dans mon sac, et le tien est dans la boîte à gants.   Yes, mine is in my bag, and yours is in the glove compartment.

J'espère que Paul et Catherine ont pris les leurs.   I hope Paul and Catherine have brought theirs.

Ne t'inquiète pas, Catherine me disait hier qu'elle venait de renouveler le sien.   Don't worry, Catherine was telling me yesterday that she has just renewed hers.

 The last example above should remind you that **le sien** means *his* or *hers* depending on the gender of the owner. In this case it means *hers* (Catherine's). **Le sien** is masculine because it stands for **passeport**.

 Not all uses of *mine*, *yours*, etc. in English will be expressed using **le mien**, etc. in French. In the following common cases you would not use **le mien**:

C'est à moi.	It's mine.
Un de mes amis m'a téléphoné.	A friend of mine telephoned me.
	(*one of my friends* . . .)

The first example is very common. It identifies the owner/ emphasizes ownership, while **le mien** tends to contrast *yours/mine*, etc.

21j   *Relative pronouns*

(i)   Use

A relative pronoun relates a clause in a sentence back to the noun. The noun is referred to as the *antecedent*, and the clause introduced by a relative pronoun is called a *relative clause*:

Ce soir-là, le repas que Michèle avait préparé était exceptionnel.	That evening, the meal that Michèle had prepared was exceptional.

In the above sentence, the relative clause is **que Michèle avait préparé**, and its function is to give more information about **le repas**. The relative pronoun is **que** in this case (the object of **avait préparé**). Beware especially of the fact that in English, relative pronouns can take a variety of forms, and are often left out altogether: **le repas que Michèle avait préparé** can be expressed in English as "the meal *which* Michèle had prepared" or "the meal *that* Michèle had prepared" or indeed "the meal Michèle had prepared." This variety of alternatives does not exist in French.

(ii)   Qui, que

When used as a relative pronoun, **qui** is the subject of the clause it introduces, and **que** is the direct object:

La lettre qui est sur la table est de mes parents.	The letter which is on the table is from my parents. (**qui** *subject of* **est**)
La lettre que vous avez écrite est dans le journal.	The letter that you wrote is in the newspaper. (**que** *object of* **avez écrite**)
La femme qui habite cet appartement est russe.	The woman who lives in this apartment is Russian. (**qui** *subject of* **habite**)

| Ce n'est pas la femme que je cherche. | She is not the woman I(whom) I am seeking. (**que** *object of* **cherche**) |

(iii) Preposition + **qui/lequel**

After prepositions, **qui** is used for people, **lequel** for things:

| La dame *avec qui* je parlais est ma voisine. | The lady I was speaking to (with whom I was speaking) is my neighbor. |
| Le magasin *devant lequel* nous avons rendez-vous est tout près du restaurant. | The shop outside which we have arranged to meet is very close to the restaurant. |

• Note that **lequel** changes to **laquelle, lesquels, lesquelles**, according to the number and gender of the noun to which it refers. These forms also combine with the preposition **à** to produce **auquel, à laquelle, auxquels, auxquelles**:

| La lettre *à laquelle* je fais allusion... | The letter *to which* I am referring . . . |

However, when **à** refers to location, use **où** instead of **auquel**

| Le restaurant *où* nous allons... | The restaurant we are going to (to which we are going) . . . |

• The pronoun **de** also combines with **lequel** to give **duquel, de laquelle, desquels, desquelles**. The principal use of this form is in conjunction with expressions such as **à côté de** (beside); **près de** (near to); **au lieu de** (instead of):

| La voiture à côté de laquelle on était stationné... | The car next to which we were parked . . . |

The pronoun **dont** is the equivalent of **de** + relative **qui**:

| Voilà le professeur dont je te parlais. | That's the teacher I was talking to you about. (of whom I was talking to you) |

C'est le professeur dont la fille est dans la même classe que Sophie.	He is the teacher whose daughter (of whom the daughter) is in the same class as Sophie.

 The relative construction *whose* + noun leaves out the article in English. In French the article must be included.

Although **dont** is supposed only to be used when referring to people, it is now widely accepted when referring to things, in preference to **duquel**, except when following a preposition:

La maison *dont* il est propriétaire est en banlieue.	The house *of which* he is the owner is in the suburbs.

But

Voilà la maison dans le jardin *de laquelle* on a trouvé les objets volés.	There's the house in *whose* garden the stolen goods were found.

(iv)   Ce qui, ce que

The relative subject and object pronouns **qui** and **que** combine with **ce** to convey the meaning *what* (that which) in English:

Il m'a expliqué *ce qu*'il veut faire.	He has explained to me *what* he wants to do. (**ce qu'** is the object of **il veut faire**)
Je ne sais pas *ce qui* me pousse à le faire.	I don't know *what* prompts me to do it. (**ce qui** is the subject of **pousse**)

• In speech the construction **ce qui/que...c'est** is very common, and extremely useful:

***Ce qui* m'intéresse, c'est l'escalade.**	*What* interests me is rock climbing.
Et moi, *ce que* j'aime, c'est dormir!	Personally, *what* I like is sleeping!

• **Ce qui** and **ce que** are required after **tout** (all, everything):

Tout ce qu'elle a dit est vrai. Il m'a appris *tout ce que* je voulais savoir.	*Everything* she said is true. He taught me *all* I wanted to know.

Giving vent to your feelings: exclamations and interjections

22a Exclamations

Exclamations express emotions such as delight, anger, surprise, or fear. The standard exclamations are introduced by words normally used as interrogatives, and may be created with whatever vocabulary is apppropriate.

• Before noun phrases, **quel** is the standard device:

Quelle catastrophe!	What a disaster!
Quel beau spectacle!	What a fine spectacle!
Quel bruit!	What a noise!
Quels voisins!	What neighbors!

• Before adjectives or adverbs, use **Que**, or more colloquially **Qu'est-ce que**.

Que c'est cher!	Isn't it expensive!
Qu'est-ce qu'il est bête!	How stupid he is!

• **Quoi?** and **Comment?** are both used to express surprise/incredulity:

Quoi? Tu lui as prêté ta voiture?	What? You've lent him your car?
Ça alors!	Well, I never!

There are, of course, many idiomatic and colorful exclamations in French as in other languages. In this section we have looked simply at those standard formulations that can be safely employed.

22b Interjections

Interjections range from words or short phrases that are really mild exclamations to the noises associated with emotions.

Hein?	Signifies that you would like something to be repeated, or that you don't understand.
Aïe!	Ouch!
Ah!	Expresses relief, resignation, despair, fatigue.
Atchoum!	Sneeze. Response in French is – **A tes souhaits!** or the more familiar – **A tes amours!**

E

LINKING AND MODIFYING MEANINGS: PREPOSITIONS AND ADVERBIAL EXPRESSIONS

Prepositions and their uses

23a What is a preposition?

(i) A preposition is a connecting word that is placed in front of a noun or pronoun to relate it to the rest of the sentence. Here are some examples:

Je vais partir *après* le petit déjeuner.	I'm going to leave *after* breakfast.
Je prends l'avion *à* Orly.	I'm taking a plane *at* Orly (airport).
Je voyage *avec* un collègue.	I'm traveling *with* a colleague.
Je passerai le chercher *chez* lui *vers* dix heures.	I'll call for him *at* his *home at* about ten o'clock.

(ii) Prepositional phrases

Prepositions like **de** and **à** are frequently used in French to create prepositional phrases with the value of an adjective, an adverb, or a relative clause [➤3c]:

Elle portait un chapeau *de paille*.	She was wearing a *straw* hat.
Les voitures avançaient *au pas*.	The cars were creeping forward/ (*advancing* at walking pace).
Le jeune homme *aux cheveux longs*, comment s'appelle-t-il?	The young man *with long hair*, what's his name?

(iii) Prepositions + verb

Prepositions are also used before verbs, in which case the verb is almost always in the infinitive:

Je n'ai pas téléphoné *pour* réserver nos places.	I haven't telephoned *to* reserve our seats.
On peut presque toujours avoir des places *sans* réserver.	You can almost always get seats *without* reserving.

Only the preposition **en** takes a verb form other than the infinitive, in this case the present participle [➤10b(ii)]:

En **arrivant, nous prendrons un taxi pour aller aux bureaux de notre client.**	On arrival, we will take a taxi to our client's offices.

(iv) *Verbs + prepositions; adjectives, adverbs, nouns + prepositions*

A, **de**, and **pour** are frequently used as fixed links following particular verbs [➤8f]:

J'essaie toujours *de* **voir mes clients chez eux.**	I always try to see my clients on their home ground.
Je ne réussis pas toujours *à* **le faire.**	I don't always succeed in doing that.
Elle attend *pour* **traverser.**	She is waiting to cross.

And following particular adjectives, adverbs, and nouns:

Je suis content *de* **te voir.**	I'm pleased to see you. (*adjective* **content + de**)
Je ne suis pas prêt *à* **partir.**	I'm not ready to leave. (*adjective* **prêt + à**)
J'ai trop *à* **faire...**	I have too much to do . . . (*adverb* **trop + à**)
...et je n'ai pas le temps *de* **m'organiser.**	. . . and I haven't time to get organized. (*noun* **le temps + de**)

23b   *Common prepositions and their use*

Because prepositions are used in a variety of ways, with considerable variation of meaning both within and between languages, it is generally easier to learn them in context, that is, in association with particular expressions, fixed phrases, or defined uses. The meaning in English is often the least reliable clue to the choice of the appropriate preposition in French. The following alphabetical list illustrates the range of uses and meanings of the most common prepositions and prepositional phrases:

179

(i) *A, au, aux* [➤19c]

• Destination, location, direction, position (to, at, in, on):

à la gare	at/to the station
au guichet	at/to the ticket counter
à gauche, à droite	to/on the left/right
à Strasbourg	to/at/in Strasbourg (**à** *before town names*)
au Mexique	to/at/in Mexico (**au/aux** *before masculine/plural countries but* **en** *before feminine countries* [➤23b(xiii)])
à la cuisine	to/in the kitchen
au mur	on the wall
à la télévision	on the television
à la page 2	on page 2
au chapitre 3	in Chapter 3
à cheval sur	astride
au soleil, à l'ombre	in the sun, in the shade

• Time, price, distance, speed, measure (at, in, to, until, by):

à sept heures	at seven o'clock
à minuit	at midnight
du jour au lendemain	from one day to the next
au mois de juin (*but* en juin)	in June
au début du siècle	at the beginning of the century
au printemps	in spring (*but other seasons with* **en**)
à dix francs le kilo	at ten francs a kilo
à cinq kilomètres	five kilometers away
à cent kilomètres à l'heure	at a hundred kilometers an hour
Ça se vend au litre	It is sold by the liter

[For more on numbers ➤26; for more on dates and seasons ➤28.]

• Method, means, manner, use (by, on, in, with):

chauffer au gaz, à l'électricité	to heat by gas, electricity
fait à la main	made by hand
à pied, à cheval, à bicyclette	on foot, on horseback, by bicycle
à voix haute/basse	in a loud/quiet voice
au gril, au micro-onde	on/under the grill, in the microwave
poulet aux petits pois	chicken with peas
à la sauce madère	with madeira sauce
une table à repasser	an ironing board

• Added detail or features:

l'homme à la barbe blanche	the man with the white beard
un piano à queue	grand piano (piano with a tail)
la maison aux volets verts	the house with the green shutters

• With a small number of verbs taking an indirect object in French but not in English:

| acheter à | buy from |

[For a full list ➤8e(i).]

(ii)   A côté de (beside, next to)

| Elle était assise *à côté de* son père. | She was sitting next to her father. |

Also:

| du côté de | in/from the direction of |

| Le bruit venait *du côté de* la chambre. | The sound came from the direction of the bedroom. |

(iii)   Après (after)

après le repas	after the meal
après six heures	after six o'clock
à gauche après le cinéma	on the left after the movie house
après avoir mangé	after eating (*note perfect infinitive in French but present participle in English*)
d'après	according to

| *D'après* les journaux, ils vont divorcer. | According to the newspapers, they are getting a divorce. |

(iv)   Au-dessus de (over, above)

au-dessus du lit	over the bed
au-dessus de nos têtes	above our heads
au-dessus de cent francs	over a hundred francs

[For more on **sur** ➤23b(xx); for **au-dessous de** (under) ➤23b(xix) **sous**.]

(v) *Au lieu de* (instead of)

Au lieu d'abandonner son projet, il a recruté d'autres enthousiastes.	Instead of abandoning his project, he recruited other enthusiasts.

(vi) *Avant* (before)

Avant expresses time or sequence, not position [➤23b(xii) **devant, derrière**]:

avant l'orage	before the storm
avant les autres	before the others
à droite avant la poste	on the right before the post office
avant de payer/partir, etc.	before paying/leaving, etc.

(vii) *Avec* (with)

Je vais avec vous.	I'm going with you.
Je le sers avec du riz.	I serve it with rice.

[For other equivalents of "with" ➤23b(i).]

(viii) *Chez*

• At someone's house or place:

Elle vient de chez les Dumont.	She has come from the Dumonts' (house).
Elle est maintenant chez le boucher.	She is now at the butcher's.
Après, elle passe chez le pharmacien.	After that, she is going to the pharmacist's.

• In the case of:

Chez Jean-Paul, on n'est jamais sûr.	With Jean-Paul you can never be sure.

(ix) *Dans*

• In, into, from (*place, content*):

dans l'église	in/into the church
dans ce programme	in this programme

dans mon journal	in my newspaper
dans le nord	in the north

J'ai pris une chemise dans l'armoire.	I took a shirt from the wardrobe.

[For use of "in" with countries and regions ➤23b(xi).]

• In (*time*):

Le film commence dans cinq minutes.	The movie starts in five minutes.

 Dans + time means "at the end of." In the above example, the movie will start at the end of five minutes, or in five minutes' time. **En** + time means time taken for something to happen:

Nous ferons la descente en une heure.	We will complete the descent in an hour.

(x) De [also du, des ➤19d]

• Possession/definition:

le frère de Marie	Marie's brother
le coin du jardin	the corner of the garden
le chemin du village	the road to the village
le train de Paris	the train to Paris, the Paris train
les vacances de mi-trimestre	the half-term vacations
le Jour de l'An	New Year's day

• After expressions of quantity:

beaucoup de lettres	many letters
une paire de gants	a pair of gloves
une douzaine de bouteilles	a dozen bottles
un verre d'eau	a glass of water
trop de sommeil	too much sleep

• From:

Il vient d'Espagne/du Canada/des Antilles.	He comes from Spain/Canada/the West Indies.

[For details of other prepositions with names of countries ➤23b(i), (ii).]

du matin au soir	from morning to night
Le livre est différent du film.	The book is different from the movie.
Il est originaire de Marseille.	He originates from Marseille.

• With, in (manner):

d'une façon désagréable	in an unpleasant way
d'une voix douce	in a gentle voice
d'une manière bizarre	in an odd way
d'un air méfiant	with an air of distrust

• By, with (agent):

couvert de boue	covered with mud
entouré de maisons	surrounded by houses
peuplé d'oiseaux	inhabited by birds
rempli de chiffres	filled with figures
inondé de demandes	flooded with requests
accablé de chaleur	overwhelmed by heat

• After **quelqu'un**, **quelque chose**, **rien**, **personne**, etc.:

quelqu'un d'important	someone important
quelque chose de joli	something pretty
rien de grave	nothing serious
personne de ma connaissance	nobody I know

> [For **de** linking verb with infinitive ➤8f; for **de** after superlatives➤20h.]

(xi) Depuis

• Since, for (time):

Il n'a pas mangé depuis hier.	He hasn't eaten since yesterday.
Il dort depuis deux heures.	He has been asleep for two hours.

> [See also **pendant** (for) ➤23b(xvi); for use of tenses with **depuis** ➤12a(iv).]

• From (places):

Depuis ma fenêtre, je vois les Alpes.	From my window I can see the Alps.

(xii) **Devant** *(in front of)*; **derrière** *(behind)*

Devant expresses position not sequence[➤23b(vi) **avant**]:

On s'est donné rendez-vous devant le cinéma.	We arranged to meet outside the movie house.
Devant moi, le panorama était sensationnel.	The view before me was terrific.
Les enfants sont installés devant la télévision.	The children are settled in front of the television.
Il y a un robinet derrière le garage.	There's a faucet/tap behind the garage.

(xiii) **En**

En fulfils a variety of prepositional functions in French, alongside other all-purpose words like **à**, **de**, and **pour**. Making the correct choice between these prepositions is often difficult: as far as possible it is best to learn them in fixed phrases.

Insofar as it has a regular value, **en** expresses a generalized meaning *in*, as opposed to **dans**, which is used principally to convey physical location or destination [➤23b(ix)]. However, it frequently appears in fixed phrases where it has no separate meaning.

• In (time):

en janvier, février, etc. (*but* **au mois de janvier, etc.**)	in January, February, etc.
en été, en automne, en hiver (*but* **au printemps** ➤23b(i))	in summer, fall/autumn, winter
en 1995/ en l'an 1995	in 1995
en début de matinée	at the beginning of the morning
en fin d'après-midi	at the end of the afternoon
en deux minutes (*but* ➤23b(vii) **dans**)	in two minutes
en ce moment	at the moment

[For time, dates, seasons ➤26, 28.]

• Languages:

en russe, espagnol, japonais, etc.	in/into Russian, Spanish, Japanese etc.
de français en anglais	from French to English

PREPOSITIONS AND ADVERBIALS

• Countries:

En is used to convey *to, in* before names of countries, regions, and continents, where these are feminine singular nouns (which most are; ➤18d):

Nous partons en Espagne.	We're off to Spain.
Nous avons une villa en Catalogne.	We have a villa in Catalonia.

Where names of countries etc. are masculine (or plural feminine) use **au, aux**:

Nous partons aux Etats-Unis.	We're off to the United States.
Nous avons beaucoup d'amis en Amérique du nord surtout au Canada.	We have a lot of friends in North America, especially in Canada.

Dans is used, however, with names of French *départements* and with regions designated by points of the compass:

Je travaille dans la Nièvre.	I work in the Nièvre. (a *département* in the center of France)
Il y a beaucoup de chômage dans l'est.	There's a lot of unemployment in the east.

• Transport:

[See also **à**, 23b(i) and **par**, 23b(xv).]

en voiture/ en auto	by car
en moto	by motorbike
en vélo	by bicycle
en avion	by air
en train	by train

• Shape, color, material:

un vol de canards en V	a V-shaped flight of ducks
un pull en rose clair	a sweater in pale pink
un fauteuil en chêne	an oak armchair

• Before a verb:

Unlike most prepositions that are followed by the infinitive, **en** is always followed by the present participle:

en attendant mon train...   while waiting for my train . . .
en arrivant chez moi...   (on) arriving home . . .
en roulant très vite...   by driving very fast . . .

[➤10b(ii) for further details of **en** + present participle.]

(xiv) Envers ➤ vers

(xv) Par

Although the basic meaning of **par** is "by," it has a variety of uses in French and several other equivalent meanings in English.

• After passives [➤15]:

Elle a été convaincue par son père.	She was convinced /persuaded by her father.

• After **commencer** and **finir**:

Elle a commencé par nous féliciter.	She began by congratulating us.
Nous avons fini par la croire.	We ended up believing her.

[For **commencer** and **finir** with **à** or **de** ➤8f.]

• By means of, through, via:

Par le train, **par avion**, and **par le métro** can be used instead of **en train**, **en avion**, **en métro**.

par l'autoroute   by the highway
par le chemin le plus court   by the shortest route
par la N 183   via the N183
par Nantes   via Nantes
par la fenêtre/la porte, etc.   through the window/door, etc.

• Per:

une fois par jour   once a day (once per day)
50 francs par personne   50 francs per head

but

dix pour cent   ten percent

[For prices, weights, and measures ➤19c(iv).]

• The following are also useful:

par politesse	out of politeness
par terre	on/to the ground
par un beau jour d'été	on a fine summer's day

(xvi) *Pendant*

• During:

Pendant notre séjour, nous allons faire du ski.	During our stay, we are going to do some skiing.
L'accident est arrivé pendant la nuit.	The accident happened during the night.

• For:

Au mois de juin, j'ai été malade pendant quinze jours.	In June I was sick for two weeks.

It is easy to confuse the use of **pendant** and **depuis** [➤12a(iv), 23b(xi)] when expressing the English concept "for a period of time." **Pendant** is used when referring to a period of time completed in the past, while **depuis** implies a period of time running up to the present and not necessarily completed:

Je souffre depuis un mois.	I've been suffering for a month (*and still am*).
J'ai souffert pendant un mois.	I suffered for a month (*but it's over now*).

(xvii) *Pour* (for)

Pour is equivalent to a range of meanings of "for" in English:

Voilà un cadeau pour toi.	Here is a present for you.
Je travaille pour un groupe international.	I work for an international group.
Il faut être là pour trois heures.	We have to be there for three o'clock.

Je vais en France pour trois semaines.	I'm going to France for three weeks. (*intended period of stay*) [**>pendant** 23b(xvi), **depuis** 12a(iv), 23b(xi)]
J'en ai pour une demi-heure.	I'll be another half-hour/I have another half hour. (*of whatever I'm doing*)

• **Pour** + infinitive:

Pour is sometimes useful when linking a main verb to a following infinitive, with the sense of "in order to," "with the intention of":

Je reste ici pour surveiller les enfants.	I'm staying here to keep an eye on the children.

But the idea of intention is frequently conveyed without **pour**, especially when verbs of movement are involved:

Nous sommes allés le chercher à la gare.	We went to fetch him from the station.

Pour is also used with the perfect infinitive in the sense of "for having":

Je l'ai remercié *pour avoir donné* son temps.	I thanked him *for having given* his time.
Je lui en veux *pour avoir abandonné* ses enfants.	I have a grudge against him *for abandoning* his children.

 Attendre, "to wait (for)," can cause particular problems for English-speaking learners of French. In its basic form it is not followed by **pour,** but takes a direct object:

Elle attend le bus.	She is waiting for the bus.

Nor is **pour** required when stating the length of time she waits:

Elle attend dix minutes.	She waits (for) ten minutes.

However, when **Elle attend** is followed by an infinitive, to convey the idea "waiting to do something," it is necessary to use **pour**:

Elle attend pour traverser.	She is waiting to cross the road.

(xviii) Près de (near to)

Elle a un appartement près de la gare.	She has a flat near the station.

(xix) Sous (under)

sous les ponts de Paris...	under the bridges of Paris . . .
sous peine de mort	under pain of death
sous l'influence de son mari	under her husband's influence
sous la pluie	in the rain

Note also **au-dessous de** (underneath, below):

Au-dessous de la moquette, il y a des vieux journaux.	Under the carpet there are old newspapers.
Je ne vends pas cette maison au-dessous de trois cent mille francs.	I'm not selling this house for less than three hundred thousand francs.

(xx) Sur

• On (position):

[➤23b(i) for **à** used to convey "on."]

sur le buffet	on the sideboard
l'un(e) sur l'autre	the one on top of the other
les un(e)s sur les autres	on top of one another
sur votre gauche	on your left
J'ai dix francs sur moi.	I've ten francs on me.

• Other uses:

Je l'ai lu sur mon journal.	I read it in the newspaper.
La clé est sur la porte.	The key is in the door.

Un jardin de trente mètres sur dix.	A yard/garden thirty meters by ten.
On m'a donné dix sur vingt.	I was given ten out of twenty.
J'étais sur le point d'accepter.	I was on the point of accepting.

[➤23b(iv) for more on ***au-dessus de***.]

(xxi) Vers, envers

• For place, time, use **vers:**

Il allait vers la piscine.	He was going toward the swimming pool.
C'était vers neuf heures du soir.	It was about nine in the evening.
On était vers la fin du programme.	We were near the end of the program.

• For "toward," expressing attitude, feelings, etc., use **envers:**

Son attitude envers moi est désagréable.	His attitude toward me is unpleasant.

24 Types of adverbial expression

24a What is an adverbial expression?

(i) Adverbial expressions are words or groups of words that modify the meanings of verbs, adjectives, or other adverbs. Adverbial expressions (often shortened to *adverbials*) can take the form of a single word, a phrase, or a complete clause with its own verb:

Il va commencer son discours.	He is going to begin his speech.
Il va commencer son discours *immédiatement.*	(immediately: *adverb*)
Il va commencer son discours *dans quelques secondes*.	(in a few seconds: *adverbial phrase*)
Il va commencer son discours *quand je lui ferai signe*.	(when I give him the signal: *adverbial clause*)

Each of these three adverbials performs the same sort of function, of modifying the meaning of **il va commencer** by adding information, in this case about when the action will happen. The word **immédiatement** is itself an adverb, but the adverbial phrase and the adverbial clause are simply groups of words performing the same role. [For the difference between phrase and clause ►4e.]

(ii) *Adverb + adjective or adverb*

Adverbs can modify verbs, as in the above illustration, but also adjectives and other adverbs:

Le toit est complètement neuf.	The roof is completely new. (**complètement** *modifies* **neuf**)
Le toit est presque complètement neuf.	The roof is almost completely new. (**presque** *modifies* **complètement**)

24b *Formation of adverbs*

(i) *Adverbs formed from adjectives*

The majority of adverbs in French (as in English) are formed from adjectives; **-ment** is added to the feminine singular form of the adjective:

Adjective	*Feminine*	*Adverb*	
complet	**complète**	**complètement**	completely
froid	**froide**	**froidement**	coolly, coldly
sec	**sèche**	**sèchement**	drily
heureux	**heureuse**	**heureusement**	happily

• Some adjectives ending in a vowel form their adverb from the masculine:

vrai	vraiment
poli	poliment

• Most adjectives ending in **-ant** or **-ent** form their adverb with **-amment, -emment**:

prudent	**prudemment**	carefully
récent	**récemment**	recently
constant	**constamment**	constantly
courant	**couramment**	currently

The only important exception is **lent, lentement** (slowly).

• Some adjectives change the final **-e** of the feminine form to **-é** to form the adverb, as a reflection of the pronunciation:

Adjective	*Feminine*	*Adverb*	
aveugle	**aveugle**	**aveuglément**	blindly
commun	**commune**	**communément**	communally
confus	**confuse**	**confusément**	confusedly
énorme	**énorme**	**énormément**	enormously
intense	**intense**	**intensément**	intensely
précis	**précise**	**précisément**	precisely
profond	**profonde**	**profondément**	deeply

• Some adverbs are formed from their adjectives in a wholly irregular way:

bon	**bien**	well
bref	**brièvement**	briefly
gentil	**gentiment**	kindly
mauvais	**mal**	badly

meilleur	**mieux**	better, best
moindre	**moins**	less, least
petit	**peu**	little

• A small number of adjectives have no adverb derived from them. These include **content** (pleased), **charmant** (charming), and **fâché** (angry). It is worth remembering that this illogicality occurs also with some words in other languages, for example, there is no adverb from *difficult* in English ("difficultly"?). In such cases, it is perfectly simple to use an adverbial phrase to express the meaning:

Elle m'a souri d'un air très content.	She smiled at me very contentedly.

 Vite (quickly), does not exist as an adjective.

• Adjectives are used as adverbs in a limited range of fixed expressions:

parler bas/fort/haut	speak quietly/loudly/audibly
coûter/payer cher	cost/pay a lot of money (dearly)
couper court	cut short
travailler dur	work hard
sonner faux	have a false ring
chanter faux	sing out of tune
refuser net	refuse point blank

Note also **soudain**, which is used in the same form as an adjective (sudden) and more frequently as an adverb (suddenly).

(ii) Adverbs not formed from adjectives

Many of the commonest adverbs, especially those answering the questions *When?* and *Where?* are not formed from adjectives. These are often short words such as **ici** (here), **là** (there), **bientôt** (soon), **déjà** (already), **ainsi** (thus), **dedans** (inside). In many cases, common words are used as adverbs, prepositions, or conjunctions in different settings:

J'ai dormi après le repas.	I slept after the meal. (**après** *is a preposition*)
J'ai travaillé après.	I worked afterward. (**après** *is an adverb*)

(iii) *Comparison of adverbs*

The comparative and superlative of adverbs in French are formed in much the same way as adjectives [➤20h], by the use of **plus**, **le plus**, **moins**, **le moins**:

Adverb	Comparative	Superlative
fréquemment	**plus fréquemment**	**le plus fréquemment**
frequently	more frequently	the most frequently
	moins fréquemment	**le moins fréquemment**
	less frequently	the least frequently

Since, unlike adjectives, adverbs do not agree with the words they modify, the article in the superlative **le plus** is always **le**, never **la** or **les**, as with adjectives.

As with adjectives, a small number of adverbs have irregular comparatives and superlatives:

bien   well   **mieux**   better   **le mieux**   the best

Moi je ne chante pas bien. Ma femme chante mieux que moi, mais dans la famille c'est ma fille qui chante le mieux.	I'm not a good singer (I don't sing well). My wife sings better than I, but in our family my daughter is the one who sings the best.

beaucoup   much   **plus**   more   **le plus**   the most

Qui voyage le plus, Philippe ou Claudine? Je sais qu'ils se déplacent beaucoup tous les deux, mais il faut aussi que je sache si Philippe voyage plus que sa collègue.	Who travels the most, Philippe or Claudine? I know they both move around a lot, but I have to know whether Philippe travels more than his colleague.

Note that when **plus** is used on its own in this way as an adverb, the final **-s** is pronounced. The **-s** is also pronounced when **plus** is used to mean "plus" (+) in English.

Ce soir nous serons cinq, plus les trois enfants.	There will be five of us this evening, plus the three children.

peu   little   **moins**   less   **le moins**   the least

These are used in exactly the same way as **plus** in the above examples.

 The adverb corresponding to **pire** (worse) (the comparative form of **mauvais** ➤20h) is **pis**, but it is rarely used except in fixed expressions such as **tant pis!** (too bad!).

24c Position of adverbs

(i) Verb + adjective or adverb

When an adverb modifies an adjective or another adverb, it is placed immediately in front of it, as in English:

totalement faux	totally false
très souvent	very often
tout près	very close

(ii) Verb + adverb

When it modifies a verb, an adverb is usually placed immediately after the verb, often in marked contrast to English, which places adverbs in a variety of positions:

Elle *conduit prudemment* la voiture de son mari.	She *drives* her husband's car *carefully*.
Elle *conduit souvent* en ville.	She *often drives* in town.

(iii) Compound tenses

In the case of compound tenses, the adverb usually follows the past participle:

Nous avons trouvé facilement l'adresse.	We found the address easily.

However, a number of commonly used adverbs such as **bien**, **beaucoup**, **trop**, **peu**, **souvent**, **bientôt**, **déjà** are placed after the auxiliary:

J'ai déjà vu ce film.	I've seen this movie already.
Il m'a beaucoup plu.	I liked it a lot (it pleased me much).

㉕ Negatives

25a Words of negation

The following words convey negation in French:

pas	not
jamais	never, not ever
rien	nothing, not anything
personne	nobody, no one, not anyone/anybody
nulle part	nowhere, not anywhere
nul	no, not any
nullement	in no way, not in any way
ni	neither, nor
plus	no more, no longer, not any more, not any longer
aucun	no, none, not one
guère	hardly

25b Making verbs negative

(i) **Ne** + negative term

Verbs are made negative by using the above list of negative terms together with the word **ne**, which is placed before the verb and before any object pronouns [➤21b(v)] that may be present:

Je ne serai pas là ce soir.	I won't be there this evening.
Ils ne m'invitent jamais en semaine – ils savent que je suis souvent en déplacement.	They never invite me on a weekday – they know I'm often away.

(ii) Negatives in compound tenses

In compound tenses, the negatives **pas**, **jamais**, **rien**, **guère**, normally follow the auxiliary:

Nous n'avons *pas* fixé les dates de nos vacances.	We haven't fixed our vacation dates.
Nous n'avons *rien* décidé pour cette année.	We haven't decided *anything* for this year.

Moi, je n'ai *guère* eu le temps d'y penser...	I've *hardly* had time to give it any thought . . .
...et mon mari n'a *jamais* été si occupé.	. . . and my husband has *never* been so busy.

• **Personne** and **nulle part** normally come after the past participle in compound tenses:

Je n'ai rencontré *personne* dans la rue.	I met *no one* in the street.
Je n'ai vu *nulle part* les dégâts dont on m'avait parlé.	I didn't see *anywhere* the damage I had been told about.

 In English there are generally two or more alternative wordings to express a particular negative idea using a verb:

I *never* go there	I saw *no one.*
I *don't ever* go there.	I did *not* see *anyone.*

These alternatives do not exist in French. Indeed, in French the double negative is perfectly correct in most cases, except that **pas** is *never* used with other negatives:

Il n'y a *jamais personne* à cette heure-ci.	There is *never anyone* (here) at this time. (*literally* never no one)

(iii) *Negatives as the subject of a verb*

The negatives **personne** and **rien** can stand as the subject of a verb:

J'ai sonné, mais *personne* n'est venu.	I rang the bell, but *nobody* came.

***Rien* ne bougeait derrière la porte.**	There was no movement behind the door. (*literally* nothing moved)

 There is no **pas** after verbs whose subject is already a negative. See also **ni** and **aucun**, below.

(iv) *Ni*

Ni is most frequently used to couple negative items:

Il ne parle *ni* français *ni* espagnol.	He speaks neither French nor Spanish.

In view of the emphatic effect of **ni...ni...** any pronouns that would otherwise be in normal object or subject form must be in the emphatic form [disjunctive pronoun ➤21f].

Ni *lui* ni sa femme ne sont catholiques.	Neither *he* nor his wife is Catholic. (*note verb generally plural after ni...ni...*)
Je ne reconnaîtrais ni *elle* ni sa fille.	I wouldn't recognize *her* or her daughter.

When used to couple verbs, the **ne** should be repeated:

Il *ne* téléphone ni *n'*écrit.	He neither phones nor writes.

 "Nor" used on its own in English corresponds to **non plus** in French:

Tu n'as pas vu mon parapluie? Moi *non plus*.	You haven't seen my umbrella? *Nor* have I.

(v) *Ne...plus*

Ne...plus can be used in relation to time:

Il *ne* souffre *plus* de maux de tête.	He *no longer* suffers from headaches.

Or in expressions of quantity:

Tu *n'*as *plus* de cigarettes? Non, je *n'*en ai *plus*.	Haven't you any more cigarettes? No, I haven't (any more).

[➤25b(iii) for **non plus**.]

(vi) Aucun

Aucun can be used as an adjective or a pronoun, and has a feminine form (**aucune**):

***Aucun* candidat ne s'est présenté.**	*No* candidate presented himself.
***Aucun* ne s'est présenté.**	*None* presented himself.
Je n'ai *aucune* idée.	I've *no* idea.

(vii) Nullement

Nullement (in no way) is used mainly to qualify adjectives or adverbs in a sentence:

Il *n'*est *nullement* nécessaire de changer les règles.	It's *in no way* necessary to change the rules.

(viii) Negatives with infinitives

When negating infinitives some negatives (**pas**, **jamais**, **rien**, **plus**) are placed with **ne** immediately before the infinitive:

Je lui ai dit de *ne pas* me cacher la vérité.	I told her *not* to hide the truth from me.
Elle m'a demandé de *ne jamais* révéler son secret à ma famille.	She asked me *never* to reveal her secret to my family.
On nous a conseillé de *ne rien* payer avant de recevoir les billets.	We have been advised to pay *nothing* before we receive the tickets.
On risquerait de *ne plus* revoir notre argent.	We would risk *not* seeing our money *again*.

However, where **rien** and **jamais** are used with *perfect* infinitives, they may be placed around the auxiliary infinitive **avoir** or **être**, or they may be placed together in front, in which case the effect is more emphatic:

Je suis sûr de *n'*avoir *rien* payé. **Je suis sûr de *ne rien* avoir payé.** }	I'm sure I paid *nothing*.

Other negatives, such as **personne**, **nul**, **nulle part**, **aucun**, **ni**, are placed after the infinitive:

Elle a décidé de *ne* **parler à** *personne*.	She has decided *not* to speak to *anyone*.

25c Negatives other than with verbs

(i) Non, pas

Both **non** and **pas** are used to negate the phrase that follows them. **Pas** tends to be the norm in everyday speech, while **non** is used more widely in the written language and in fixed expressions:

–Range tes affaires dans le placard, *pas* **par terre!**	Put your things away in the closet, *not* on the floor!
Non **seulement la police mais aussi le public est responsable.**	*Not* only the police but also the public is responsible.

Non pas can be used for added emphasis:

Cette peinture est bleue et *non* **pas grise.**	This paint is blue *rather than* gray.

(ii) Other negatives

• **Jamais**, **personne**, and **rien** frequently stand on their own, often with the rest of the sentence implied:

–Il y a beaucoup de monde sur le quai? –Non, *personne*.	Are there many people on the platform? —No, *nobody*.
–Que se passe-t-il? *Rien* **de grave, j'espère.**	What's going on? *Nothing* serious, I hope.
–Tu vois souvent tes cousins? Non, *jamais*.	Do you often see your cousins? No, *never*.

Jamais can be equivalent to both "never" and "ever" in English according to context:

PREPOSITIONS AND ADVERBIALS

–*Jamais* devant les enfants!	*Never* in front of the children!
–Est-ce que vous avez *jamais* travaillé à l'étranger?	Have you *ever* worked abroad?

- Negatives such as **jamais**, **rien**, **personne**, **aucun**, **plus** are used after **sans** (without), very often before an infinitive:

sans jamais	without ever	**sans aucun**	without any
sans rien	without anything	**sans plus**	without any more
sans personne	without anybody		

Je passe tous les jours devant chez eux *sans jamais* les voir.	I go past their house every day *without ever* seeing them.
Sans aucune trace...	*Without any* trace . . .

25d Negatives in speech

It is commonplace (though not strictly correct) in everyday speech for the **ne** in negatives to be omitted, mainly with the **je** and **tu** forms of the verb, and with **c'est**:

–Je t'entends pas!	"I can't hear you!"
–J'ai pas le souvenir d'avoir payé.	"I don't remember paying."
–C'est pas possible!	"It's not possible!"

25e Ne without the value of a negative
(i) Ne...que

Equivalent to "only" in English, this widely used construction needs care in that the **que** has to be placed immediately before the word to which it refers, whereas in English the word "only" is often out of position in everyday usage:

Je ne vois qu'une erreur.	I can only see one mistake /I can see only one mistake.

- Where the **que** is followed by a personal pronoun, the emphatic (disjunctive) form is required [disjunctive pronouns ➤21f]:

Je *n'*ai parlé *qu'*à elle.	I spoke *only* to her.

• Although mostly used before nouns or pronouns, **ne...que** can be used with verbs, in the construction **ne faire que** + infinitive. In this case the English equivalent is likely to be "nothing but."

Il *ne* fait *que* se plaindre.	He does *nothing but* complain.
Je *n'*ai fait *que* rire!	I *only* laughed!

• **Ne...que** can itself be made negative:

Il *n'*y a *pas qu'*un seul moyen de le faire	There isn't just one way of doing it.

(ii) *Nonnegative use of* ***ne***

In the following expressions involving a subjunctive, **ne** appears but without any negative force:

• After verbs and expressions of fearing:

J'ai peur qu'ils *n'*arrivent avant nous.	I fear they will arrive before us.

•After **avant que** (before) and **à moins que** (unless):

Nous sortirons, à moins qu'il *ne* pleuve.	We'll go out unless it rains.

It is worth noting that these expressions tend to be those of more formal speech. For example, the last sentence above would in all probability be expressed differently in everyday language:

Nous sortirons s'il ne pleut pas.	We'll go out if it doesn't rain.

[For the use of the subjunctive ➤14.]

25f   *Si after negative questions*

Si exists as an alternative to **oui** for "yes." It is an emphatic form, and is used only when correcting or contradicting a negative statement or question:

Tu n'as pas vu la programme?	You didn't see the program?
Si, Si.	Yes, I did.
Vous n'avez pas payé.	You haven't paid.
Mais si!	But of course I have!

F

USING NUMBERS

Numerals

26a   Counting: cardinal numbers

The cardinal numbers in French are:

0	zéro	
1	un, une	*see note (i)*
2	deux	
3	trois	
4	quatre	
5	cinq	*see note (ix)*
6	six	*see note (viii)*
7	sept	
8	huit	*see notes (ix) and (xi)*
9	neuf	
10	dix	*see note (viii)*
11	onze	*see note (xi)*
12	douze	
13	treize	
14	quatorze	
15	quinze	
16	seize	
17	dix-sept	
18	dix-huit	*see note (ix)*
19	dix-neuf	
20	vingt	*see note (x)*
21	vingt et un(e)	*see notes (i) and (x)*
22	vingt-deux	*see note (x)*
23	vingt-trois	*see note (x)*
24	vingt-quatre	*see note (x)*
30	trente	
31	trente et un(e)	*see note (i)*
32	trente-deux	
40	quarante	
50	cinquante	
60	soixante	
70	soixante-dix	*see notes (iii) and (viii)*
71	soixante et onze	

72	soixante-douze	
73	soixante-treize	
74	soixante-quatorze	
75	soixante-quinze	
76	soixante-seize	
77	soixante-dix-sept	
78	soixante-dix-huit	
79	soixante-dix-neuf	
80	quatre vingts	*see note (iii)*
81	quatre-vingt-un(e)	*see notes(i) and (ii)*
82	quatre-vingt-deux	
90	quatre-vingt-dix	*see notes (iii) and (viii)*
91	quatre-vingt-onze	
100	cent	*see note (iv)*
101	cent un(e)	*see notes (i) and (v)*
102	cent deux	*see note (v)*
200	deux cents	*see note (ii)*
201	deux cent un(e)	*see notes (i) and (ii)*
202	deux cent deux	*see note (ii)*
300	trois cents	
1000	mille	*see note (iv)*
1001	mille un(e)	*see notes (i) and (v)*
1002	mille deux	
2000	deux mille	*see note (vi)*
1 000 000	un million	*see note (vii)*
1 500 000	un million cinq cent mille	
2 000 000	deux millions	
1 000 000 000	un milliard	*see note (vii)*
1 000 000 000 000	un billion	*see note (vii)*

(i) **Un** changes to **une** before a feminine noun:

Vingt et une adresses.	Twenty-one addresses.

(ii) There is no **-s** on the plural of **vingt** or **cent** if they are followed by other numbers:

quatre-vingts hommes	*but*	**quatre-vingt-cinq hommes**
deux cents francs	*but*	**deux cent cinquante francs**

USING NUMBERS

(iii)   70, 80, and 90 in Switzerland and Canada are **septante**, **octante**, and **nonante**. In Belgium, **septante** and **nonante** are used, but not **octante**.

(iv)   **Cent** and **mille** are never preceded by **un** when used as numbers:

Il y a cent invités.	There are a hundred guests.
Elle me doit mille cent francs.	She owes me one thousand one hundred francs.

(v)   There is no equivalent of the English "and" after **cent** and **mille**.

205	**deux cent cinq**
3050	**trois mille cinquante**

(vi)   **Mille** never has an **-s**, except when used to translate the English "mile":

trois mille	three thousand
trois milles	three miles

(vii)   **Un million** (million), **un milliard** (billion), and **un billion** (trillion) are all nouns. Used without additional numbers they are followed by **de**:

un million de réfugiés	a million refugees
un milliard de dollars	a billion dollars

When followed by more figures, the **de** is dropped:

Un million cinq cent mille habitants.	One million five hundred thousand inhabitants.

(viii)   The final **-x** of **six** and **dix** (alone or in other numbers):

• Is not pronounced before a consonant:

vingt-six litres

• Is pronounced **-z** before a vowel or mute **h**:

dix enfants   **six hommes**

• Is pronounced **-s** when standing alone as a number, or when otherwise placed in emphasis:

Le six a gagné – le six!	Number six is the winner – number six!
Ils arrivent le dix.	They arrive on the tenth.
Page vingt-six.	Page twenty-six.

(ix) The final consonant of **cinq** and **huit** is pronounced when the word stands alone or is otherwise placed in emphasis (and of course before a vowel or mute **h**) but is not pronounced before a consonant:

Ils habitent au quarante-cinq/huit.	They live at number 45/48. (**-q** or **-t** *pronounced*)
Ce cognac coûte cinq/huit livres de plus en Angleterre.	This brandy costs £5/£8 more in England. (**-q** or **-t** *not pronounced*)

(x) The final **-t** of **vingt** is pronounced only for the numbers 21 to 29.

(xi) When the definite article **le** is used before **huit** or **onze**, it is not reduced to **l'**.

Leur maison, c'est le huit, le neuf, le dix, ou le onze?	Is their house number 8, 9, 10, or 11?

26b Approximate numbers

(i) Cardinal number + -aine

Most approximate numbers are formed in French by adding **-aine** to the cardinal number (first dropping the final **-e** of the cardinal number, if there is one):

une dizaine	about ten (*note minor adjustment to spelling*)
une douzaine	a dozen
une quinzaine	about fifteen
une quinzaine de jours	about two weeks
une vingtaine	about twenty, a score
une trentaine	about thirty
une quarantaine	about forty
une cinquantaine	about fifty
une soixantaine	about sixty

No approximate numbers exist for 70, 80, or 90 in French.

une centaine	about a hundred
un millier	about a thousand

(ii)   *Une trentaine de,* etc.

Approximate numbers are nouns (all feminine except **un millier**) and, like other such expressions of quantity, are linked to any following words by **de**:

Elle avait une trentaine d'années.	She was about thirty.
Des centaines de maisons ont été inondées.	Hundreds of houses have been flooded.
Je l'ai vu il y a une quinzaine de jours.	I saw him about two weeks ago.

26c   *Arranging in order: ordinal numbers*

(i)   *Formation*

The ordinal numbers are formed by adding **-ième** to the cardinal number:

le septième ciel	seventh heaven
le dixième commandement	the tenth commandment
son vingt et unième anniversaire	his/her twenty-first birthday

If the cardinal number ends in **-e**, this is dropped before adding the **-ième**:

la quinzième fois	the fifteenth time

• The only major exception is **premier**, **première** (first). Note that when first is part of other numbers (such as twenty-first, one hundred and first, etc.), **premier** is not used:

le cent unième dalmatien	the one hundred and first dalmatian

Note also **cinquième** and **neuvième**, which have minor adjustments to spelling in their ordinal form.

• **Second** (feminine **seconde**) also means "second," but its use is limited to occasions where "second" is contrasted with "first," rather than occasions where it refers to the second item in a series:

Je voyage toujours en seconde (en seconde classe).	I always travel second class.

(ii)   *Ordinal numbers in use*

Ordinal numbers are not used for dates in French [➤28c], except **premier**:

le premier octobre	the first of October
le deux octobre	the second of October
le vingt et un octobre, *etc.*	the twenty-first of October, *etc.*

Nor are they used when numbers are placed after kings or others: again, except **premier**:

(le roi) Louis quatorze	(King) Louis the fourteenth
Henry Ford deux	Henry Ford the second
François premier	(King) Francis the First

In a number of common contexts, the noun to which an ordinal number refers may be omitted; for example:

Ils habitent au quinzième (au quinzième étage).	They live on the fifteenth floor.
Leur appartement est dans le seizième (dans le seizième arrondissement).	Their apartment is in the 16th district. (*Paris is divided into arrondissements*)
Leur fils est en sixième (en sixième classe) .	Their son is in the sixth grade. (*first-year secondary in the English system; last-year elementary in the American system*)

 When a cardinal number is used with **premier** or **dernier**, the cardinal number comes first—just the opposite of the order in English:

Les cinq derniers jours du mois.	The last five days of the month.
Les six premiers candidats.	The first six candidates.

[**Premier** is also used as a superlative ➤14e(ii).]

26d   Sharing out: fractions

The most commonly used fractions are:

un/le quart	a quarter
(les) trois quarts	three quarters
un/le tiers	a /one third
(les) deux tiers	two thirds
un demi	a half
la moitié	half

All other fractions are formed using ordinal numbers:

un/le huitième	an /one eighth
(les) trois cinquièmes	three fifths

Demi exists as a noun and an adjective. As a noun, it is used only as a mathematical term. As an adjective, it appears in two forms:

• As an invariable adjective preceding the noun and hyphenated to it:

une demi-bouteille	a half bottle
une demi-heure	half an hour

• Following a noun and linked to it by **et**, in which case **demi** agrees with the noun:

une bouteille et demie	a bottle and a half
une heure et demie	an hour and a half
un litre et demi	a liter and a half

Note that **la moitié** is the general word for "half" when the word carries less emphasis on the specific quantity:

J'ai passé la moitié du temps à lire.	I spent half the time reading.

Where the fraction is followed by a noun, the two are linked by **de**. In addition, if the noun is preceded by a definite article, a possessive, or a demonstrative, the fraction is also introduced by a definite article:

un quart de litre	a quarter liter

but

les trois quarts de la ville	three quarters of the town
les deux tiers de ma fortune	two thirds of my fortune
les quatre cinquièmes de cette somme	four fifths of this sum

27 Telling the time

The standard question is **Quelle heure est-il?** or **Vous auriez l'heure, s'il vous plaît?**

As in English, there are two sets of conventions for telling the time, one more traditional, the other based on the timetable use of figures. Both are widely used, and are described here.

27a   The traditional style

Il est une heure	It is one o'clock.
Il est deux heures.	It is two o'clock.
Il est trois heures, *etc.*	It is three o'clock, *etc.*
Il est quatre heures un quart. *or* **Il est quatre heures et quart** }	It is a quarter after/past four
Il est quatre heures vingt.	It is twenty past four.
Il est quatre heures et demie.	It is half past four.
Il est cinq heures moins le quart	It is a quarter to five.
Il est cinq heures moins une.	It is one minute to five.

Minuit (midnight) and **midi** (noon) are treated in the same way except that, as masculine nouns they are followed by **demi**, not **demie**, for the half hour:

Le programme termine à midi et demi.	The program ends at half past twelve.

27b   The timetable style

This style retains some features of the traditional forms:

Il est trois heures.	It is three o'clock.
Il est trois heures vingt.	It is twenty past three.

However, words such as **quart** and **demi** are discarded in favor of figures, and all figures are related to the hour before:

Neuf heures quinze	9h15
Neuf heures trente	9h30
Neuf heures quarante-cinq	9h45
Neuf heures cinquante-cinq	9h55

USING NUMBERS

 When abbreviated for written purposes, times are presented differently from English: the **h** stands for **heures**, so **9h15** is equivalent to "9:15."

• There is no French equivalent of a.m. and p.m. Where necessary, use **du matin**, **de l'après-midi**, **du soir**:

On m'a réveillé à trois heures du matin.	I was woken up at three in the morning.

• The following are useful:

Fermé de 12h15 à 14h30.	Closed from 12:15 to 2:30.
Le supermarché est ouvert jusqu'à 19h30.	The supermarket is open until 7:30 p.m.
Venez vers 8 heures.	Come around 8 o'clock.
C'est l'heure!	It's time! (*for example, to leave for the train*)
Quelle heure as-tu?	What time do you have?

The calendar

28a Days of the week

lundi	Monday	**vendredi**	Friday
mardi	Tuesday	**samedi**	Saturday
mercredi	Wednesday	**dimanche**	Sunday
jeudi	Thursday		

! Days of the week do not have capital letters in French.

• Days of the week are all masculine. The inclusion of the article changes the meaning:

Je travaille lundi.	I'm working on Monday.
Je travaille *le* lundi.	I work on Mondays.

• Note also:

aujourd'hui	today
hier	yesterday
avant-hier	the day before yesterday
demain	tomorrow
après-demain	the day after tomorrow
la veille	the day before, the previous day
le lendemain	the following day, the day after

All of these expressions, together with the days of the week, can be coupled with **matin**, **après-midi**, and **soir**:

Ils ont été cambriolés samedi soir.	They were robbed on Saturday night.
Le lendemain matin, ils ont trouvé une vitre cassée.	The next morning they found a window pane broken.

Cette nuit generally means "last night."

Je n'ai pas dormi du tout cette nuit.	I didn't sleep at all last night.

"Tonight" is **ce soir** unless it really refers to the night, in which case **cette nuit** is used:

Nous allons au cinéma ce soir.	We are going to the movies tonight.
Je vais dormir à l'hôtel cette nuit.	I'll be sleeping in a hotel tonight.

28b *Months and seasons*

janvier	January		**le printemps**	spring
février	February		**l'été**	summer
mars	March		**l'automne**	fall/autumn
avril	April		**l'hiver**	winter
mai	May			
juin	June		**en janvier**	
juillet	July		**au mois de** }	in January
août	August		**janvier**	
septembre	September		**fin janvier**	at the end of
octobre	October			January
novembre	November		**début février**	at the beginning
décembre	December			of February

 En hiver, en été, en automne, *but* **au printemps**.

28c *Dates*

Except for the first of the month, the days of the month are expressed with cardinal numbers, not ordinal numbers as in English:

le sept avril	the seventh of April
le vingt et un mars	the twenty-first of March

    but

le premier juillet	the first of July

These would normally be written **le 7 avril**, **le 21 mars**, **le 1er juillet**. No preposition is required with dates in their basic use "on" + date:

La lettre est arrivée le 3 juin et nous sommes le 10.	The letter arrived on the 3rd of June, and it's the 10th today.

Years are expressed as follows (note **mil** is sometimes used instead of **mille**):

mille neuf cent quatre-vingt treize

> *or* } 1993

dix-neuf cent quatre-vingt-treize

en 1912

> *or* } in 1912

en l'an 1912

Years are frequently shortened in everyday speech:

J'ai commencé mes études en cinquante-trois.	I started my higher education in 1953 ('53).

For identifying decades:

Dans les années trente, mes parents habitaient Paris.	In the thirties, my parents were living in Paris.

Année is usually used instead of **an**:

• After expressions of quantity with **de**, such as **combien d'années**;
• With ordinal numbers, such as **la deuxième année**;
• With approximate numbers, such as **une dizaine d'années**.

Note the following expressions:

l'année dernière/l'an dernier	last year
l'année prochaine/l'an prochain	next year

Année is used in preference to **an** when the adjective precedes the noun, which gives a different meaning:

la prochaine année	*the* next year
la dernière année	*the* last year

Note, also:

l'année suivante	the next/following year

28d Age

Age is expressed in French using the verb **avoir** + number + **ans**:

Elle a soixante-deux ans.	She is sixty-two.
Son fils a quarante ans.	Her son is forty.
Il a une fille de six mois.	He has a six month old daughter.

• In English it is normal to omit the word *years* when giving people's age, but not in French.
• Approximate numbers can be used to express age, but they must be followed by **années** instead of **ans**:

Il a une quarantaine d'années.	He is about forty.

G
INDEX

INDEX